VIKTORIA CAPEK

An Immersive Literary Journey Through TAYLOR SWIFT'S Lyrics

Illustrated by
Holly Farndell

WATKINS

Dear Reader
Viktoria Capek
Illustrated by Holly Farndell

First published in the UK and USA in 2025
by Watkins, an imprint of Watkins Media Limited
Unit 11, Shepperton House
83–93 Shepperton Road
London N1 3DF

enquiries@watkinspublishing.com

A CIP record for this book is available
from the British Library

ISBN: 978-1-78678-992-1 (Paperback)
ISBN: 978-1-78678-993-8 (eBook)

10 9 8 7 6 5 4 3 2 1

Commissioning Editor: Ella Chappell
Managing Editor: Brittany Willis
Project Manager: Gigi St John
Head of Design: Karen Smith
Illustrations: Holly Farndell
Production: Uzma Taj

www.watkinspublishing.com

Note from the Publisher: No Taylor Swift lyrics have been quoted in this journal. Space has been provided for you to write the lyrics.

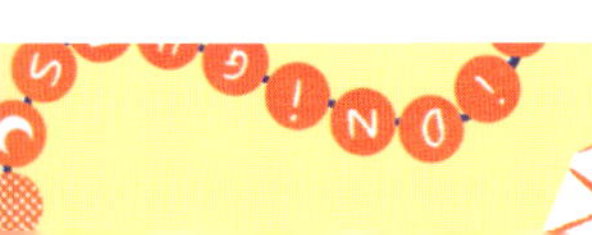

How to Use This Book

Dear Reader **is your guide to exploring the intersection of Taylor Swift's lyrics and classic literature, designed to be flexible and enjoyable for solo readers, book clubs, classrooms or casual gatherings with friends. Here's how to make the most of it:**

READ AT YOUR OWN PACE AND ORDER

You can read the chapters in any order, though I encourage starting with the Introduction to set the stage and ending with Chapter 10, which brings everything together. Each chapter stands alone, so you can dive into the ones that interest you the most.

SOLO READERS AND GROUPS WELCOME

This book works for everyone. Solo readers can treat it like a personal journal, using the questions and prompts to reflect deeply on Taylor's lyrics and their literary connections. For groups – whether it's a book club, classroom or a casual get-together – you'll find plenty of discussion points to spark conversation about Taylor's music and the referenced classic works.

WHAT IF I HAVEN'T READ THE BOOKS?

Love analysing Taylor's lyrics but don't have time to read all the literary classics? No problem! Each book mentioned comes with a crash course summary called SwiftsNotes (think CliffsNotes). These bullet points give you a quick overview of the story, so you can still engage with the connections and enjoy analysing the lyrics without missing a beat.

NOT A SWIFTIE? NO PROBLEM!

If you're more of a bookworm than a Taylor Swift fan, you'll still love this book. Every lyric is explained in context, showing how it ties into the songs and the referenced literature. You'll revisit some of your favourite novels in new ways and maybe even gain a newfound appreciation for Taylor's genius at weaving literary references into her songs.

YES, YOU CAN WRITE IN THIS BOOK!

This is a book you can write in – so grab a pen! Each chapter is packed with questions, activities and prompts designed to encourage your personal reflection and creativity.

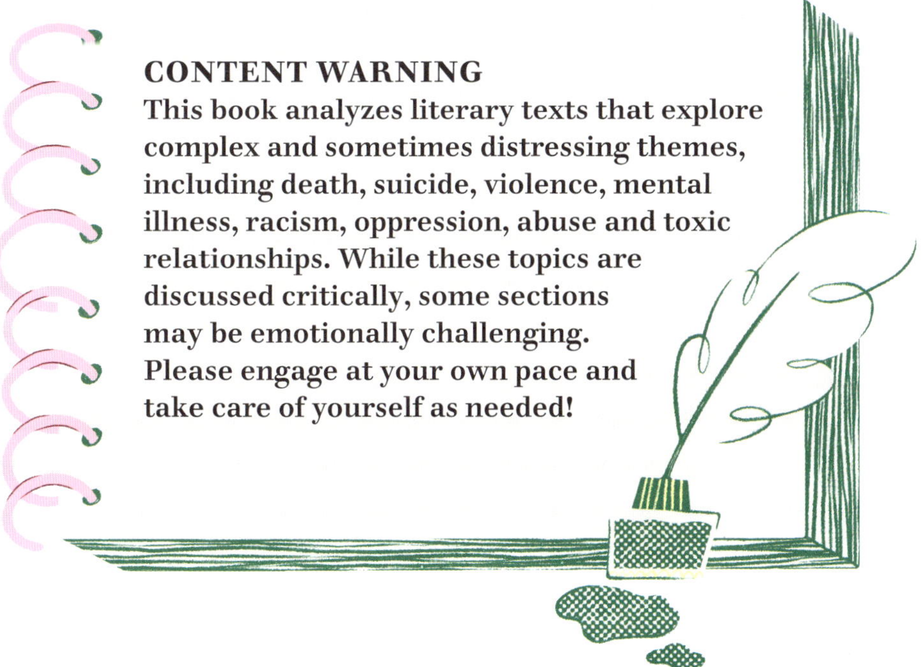

CONTENT WARNING
This book analyzes literary texts that explore complex and sometimes distressing themes, including death, suicide, violence, mental illness, racism, oppression, abuse and toxic relationships. While these topics are discussed critically, some sections may be emotionally challenging. Please engage at your own pace and take care of yourself as needed!

CHAPTER BREAKDOWN

Each chapter is organized into sections to make it easy and fun to follow.

✶ **Introduction:**
Sets the stage with an overview of the chapter's themes, books and songs

✶ **Swift Prep:**
Focus questions to warm up to the chapter's subject

✶ **SwiftsNotes:**
A summary of the literary classic, offering quick plot overviews for those who may need a refresher or are new to the book

✶ **Lyricature:**
Side-by-side comparisons of Taylor's lyrics and the literary classic, complete with quotes, activities and questions that explore both the books and the songs

✶ **Music Video Muse:**
Analyses of Taylor's music videos, drawing visual storytelling parallels to the literature

✶ **Taylor Talkback:**
A review section at the end of each chapter with reflection questions and activities to help you process everything you've learned

Whether you're exploring Taylor's lyrics, revisiting literary classics or discovering connections beyond her more obvious Easter eggs, this book is here to help you reflect, create and explore.

Introduction

Dear Reader,

You're probably reading this because you love Taylor Swift. Maybe you've cried to "this is me trying" alone in your room, or you've screamed along to "Better Than Revenge" while driving. Maybe you're in a group chat with friends that always let you know when there's a new merch drop, and you had a lot of opinions about the surprise songs Taylor sang during her Eras Tour. Maybe you share Taylor's obsession with cats. Above all, you're probably here because, in one way or another, you have connected with her music.

Taylor's music draws us in because it's relatable. Her songs are like open doors inviting us to step inside and find our own meanings. This is especially true in songs such as "All Too Well", where the emotions and experiences she describes feel so universal. The beauty of Taylor's artistry is her ability to tell her own story in a way that speaks to ours. She writes songs that feel deeply personal yet open to interpretation, making us want to explore our own feelings and experiences through her lyrics. This connection is what keeps us coming back to her music again and again, learning more about ourselves every time we listen.

And while it's true that both Taylor's relatability and honesty have always been central to her music, the way she reinvents herself from era to era – and always keeps us guessing – makes being a Swiftie quite the adventure. Part of that thrill comes from a little something this fandom knows as "Easter eggs", or the hidden messages Taylor leaves behind that make us feel like insiders to her story.

For the past 20 years, Taylor Swift has grown an army of dedicated fans equipped with the skills to dissect these Easter eggs in every musical note, lyric, video or visual she releases. The trend started in CD liner notes where Taylor would capitalize or uncapitalize certain letters to spell out secret words or phrases. We first saw Easter eggs in 2006 when her debut album was released. The printed lyrics for "Should've Said No" spelled the name "Sam" over and over again, and fans speculated it was about Taylor's high school boyfriend, Sam Armstrong. Two years later, Taylor confirmed what fans had guessed and told Women's Health magazine it was a clue leading them to who the song was about. Don't worry if you missed the "Sam" era of finding Easter eggs and connecting the dots in Taylor's songs – this book will help you read between the lines (and the liner notes) so that you never have to miss out on breaking down Taylor's songs in an exciting and meaningful way again.

As Taylor and her listeners have grown up, the Easter eggs in her music have evolved, becoming more intricate and subtle than messages in liner notes. In the song "Daylight" from her seventh album *Lover*, there's a nod to the title track from her fourth album, *Red*. They're both songs about love but in totally different ways: "Red" describes love as fiery and intense, and "Daylight" sees it as warm and steady, showing how her view of love has grown over the years. These references keep us engaged and excited to decode her lyrics. They almost feel like a scavenger hunt for what Taylor is really thinking when she writes.

The secret messages in her music videos, especially from the *Reputation* era onwards, have taken Taylor's Easter egging to a whole new level. To catch just one callout in the "Look What You Made Me Do" music video, you need to know pop culture, Shakespeare and a bit of Latin! In one scene, Taylor sits on a golden throne with the phrase "Et tu, Brute?" engraved on it. The line means, "And you, Brutus?" in English, and it's from Shakespeare's *Julius Caesar*. It's spoken by Caesar when he realises his close friend has betrayed him, similar to how Taylor went public about how Kim Kardashian and Kanye West betrayed her in 2016.

Eager to stay in the know about the songs' messages and meanings, we do our research and try our best to keep up with Taylor. But some Easter eggs planted by the mastermind herself leave us puzzled (raise your hand if her "five holes in the fence" photo still keeps you up at night).

Another tool in Taylor's arsenal is the references to classic literature and poetry sprinkled across her discography. In 2016, Taylor told Vogue that if she were a teacher, she would teach English. In 2019, she declared her love for Shakespeare to Elle. It's no surprise that in 2022, New York University recognized her with an honorary doctorate of fine arts – she is a brilliant writer influenced by other brilliant writers.

Taylor has intertwined her music with the stories we grew up reading. We see it in obvious references to classic works of literature, such as *The Scarlet Letter* in "Love Story", and in more abstract allusions in songs such as "happiness", where she sings about a Gatsby-like green light. You can really feel her affinity for written works in her later albums, including the dark and Gothic entirety of TS11 – *The Tortured Poets Department: The Anthology*. Listening to her music feels like unriddling a poem in your favourite literature class, which is a part of the fun.

With all these songs referencing a library of classic books, it'd be foolish to name this book after anything other than "Dear Reader", the cryptic, final track on Taylor's *Midnights (3am Edition)* album. The song feels like a direct conversation with her, wrapped in a synthy, ethereal ballad, and it's written like an advice column from a newspaper. In "Dear Reader", Taylor reimagines the concept with her own flair. While the song appears to offer us advice, it's also telling us that not every question requires an answer – at least not from her.

Throughout her career, Taylor's lyrics and Easter eggs have spelled out events from her life. Her early albums read like personal journal entries about family, relationships, friendships and the intricacies of growing up. *Taylor Swift* and *Fearless* offered us what felt like a window into her world.

This thread has unravelled as she has matured, and her music has become more complex. In "Dear Reader", she challenges us to stop looking to her for explanations. Instead, she invites us to find our own meanings in her lyrics and to explore the artistic parallels hidden throughout her songs.

This book offers you the opportunity to do just that by exploring the fascinating connection between Taylor's music and works of classic literature. By looking at her songs through a literary lens, we can uncover the depth of her lyrics and the richness of her many references. Rather than simply looking to her Easter eggs for explanations, we'll explore her lyrics as powerful works of storytelling that draw comparisons to *Romeo*

and Juliet, *Frankenstein*, and *Rebecca*. Her work invites us to think about the stories she tells, the characters she creates and the emotions she captures, giving listeners a deeper appreciation for the layers within her songs. And by looking at her lyrics alongside classic literature, we can uncover new ways to connect with her music – ways that make us think, feel and see her work in an entirely new light.

I invite you to take Taylor's advice and explore what these lyrics and stories mean to you, using this book as a guide. Learn about stories you love, discover new ones and revisit old favourites. Steady your mind with SwiftsNotes questions, write down your thoughts and theories, explore the links Taylor makes in her music and share your ideas with other Swifties. My hope is that your analysis of these songs turns your passion into a project, mirroring the way you interact with classic literature. I hope you enjoy using this book to deepen your understanding of Taylor's music and the timeless stories that inspire it.

Forever and always,

**All songs mentioned in this book refer to Taylor's rerecorded versions, known as "Taylor's Version", where applicable. For songs that have not yet been rerecorded, this book refers to the original versions, with the understanding that they are part of her artistic legacy. This note is made out of respect for her ongoing effort to reclaim ownership of her music.*

Who Are You, Anyway?

Before we jump (then fall) into all things Taylor, let's focus on you! Fill in the blank spaces for a bit of self-reflection before we get to the deeper stuff.

* Name:

* Age:

* Your age when you discovered Taylor Swift:

* Favourite Taylor song:

* Favourite Taylor album:

* Favourite Swift era:

✶ Top five best Taylor Swift lyrics:

1

2

3

4

5

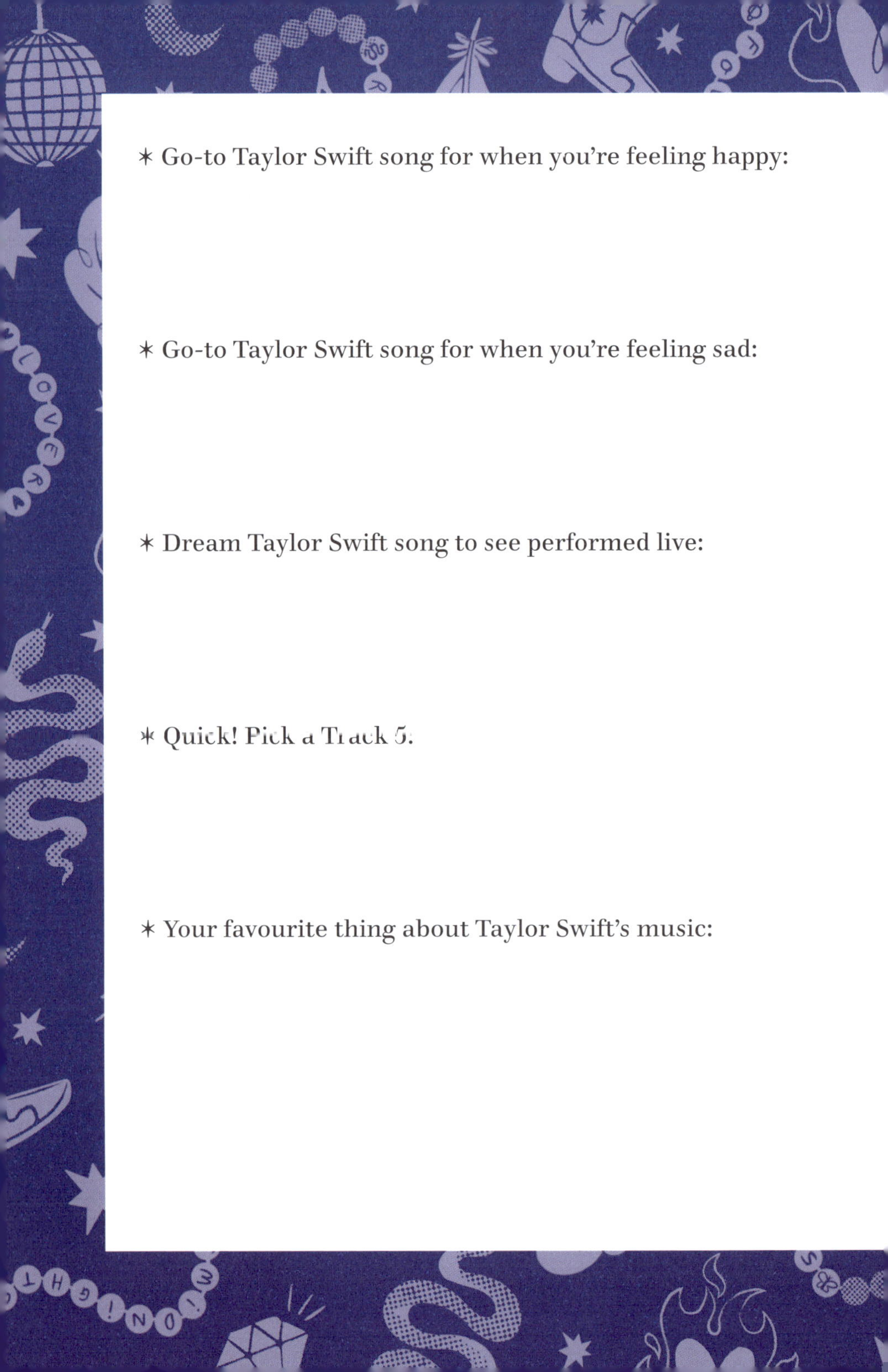

✶ Go-to Taylor Swift song for when you're feeling happy:

✶ Go-to Taylor Swift song for when you're feeling sad:

✶ Dream Taylor Swift song to see performed live:

✶ Quick! Pick a Track 5:

✶ Your favourite thing about Taylor Swift's music:

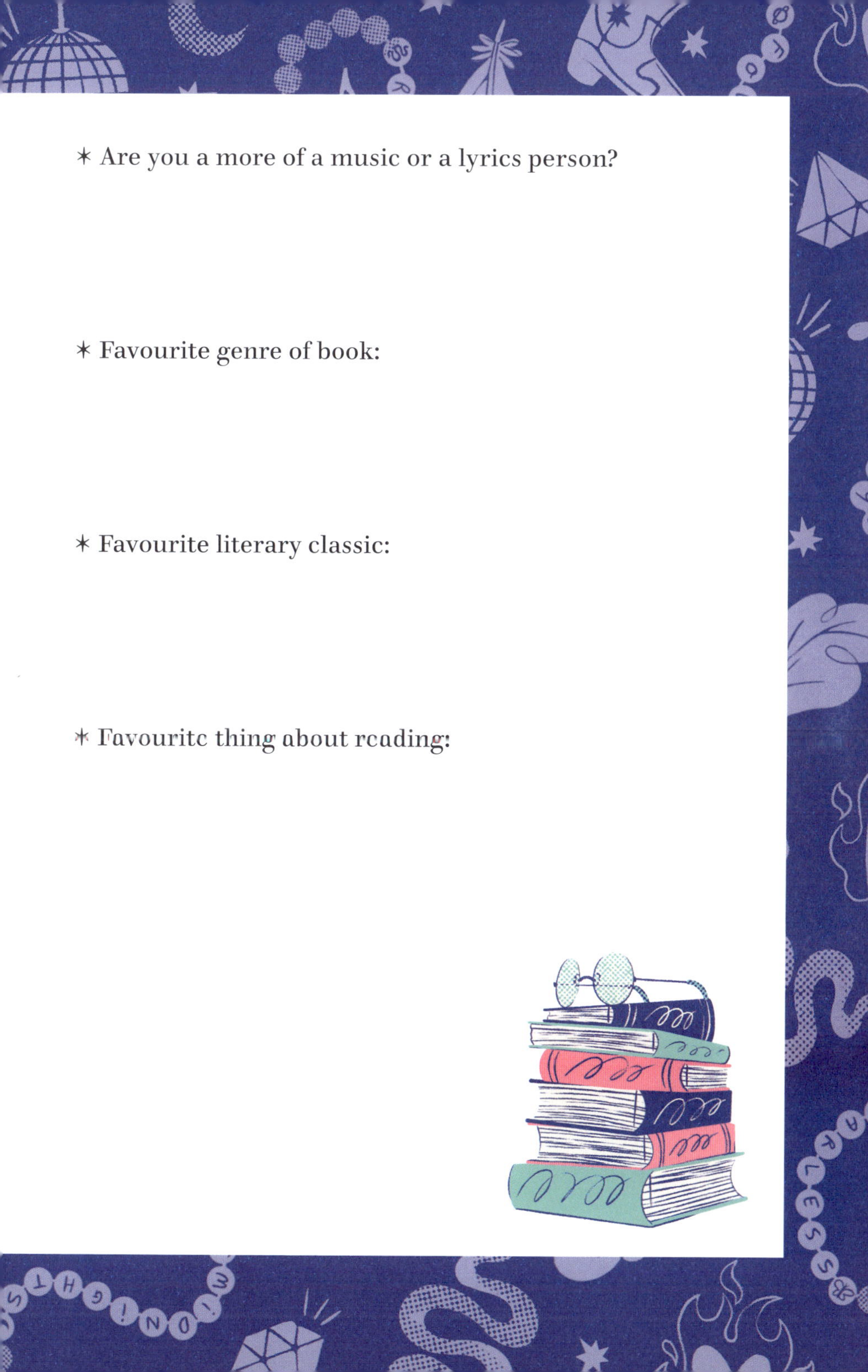

* Are you a more of a music or a lyrics person?

* Favourite genre of book:

* Favourite literary classic:

* Favourite thing about reading:

CHAPTER 1

Taylor Swift as the Ultimate Unreliable Narrator

The concept of the unreliable narrator in Taylor Swift's music

THE BOOKSHELF	THE PLAYLIST
The Great Gatsby	**"Dear Reader"**
	"Blank Space"

Queue up this chapter's songs to listen and follow along!

Meet the Unreliable Narrator

An unreliable narrator misleads their readers. Some narrators do it on purpose, and others do it without realizing they are.

This device was extremely common in 20th-century writing and was used to show audiences that a person's reality is subjective, meaning it's shaped by their own perspective, experiences and emotions. What one person sees or feels might not be the same as what someone else perceives (think "beauty is in the eye of the beholder").

Unreliable narrators are compelling because they create tension between what they say and what is "true" within the story. Readers have to question everything and dig deeper to find out what is really going on. This makes the experience more interactive because it forces the audience to put on their detective hats and piece clues together.

Being an unreliable narrator isn't necessarily a flaw – in fact, it can make a story more complex and engaging!

Understanding the unreliable narrator can help you build a deeper appreciation for Taylor's music and lyrics. This chapter explores how the lyrics in songs such as "Dear Reader" and "Blank Space" reflect traits commonly seen in unreliable narrators, similar to those in stories such as *The Great Gatsby*. We'll look at how Taylor uses this device in her music, and you'll start to discover some of the literary Easter eggs she has hidden in her songs.

Swift Prep

Let's begin with a few questions to focus your mind.

✶ Can a song's narrator be unreliable, or does this concept only apply to traditional storytelling formats, such as books and movies?

✶ Think of your favourite books, movies or TV shows. Who are the narrators, and are they just telling you their side of the story? What do those characters have in common?

✶ Can you think of any of Taylor's songs where she might not be telling you the whole story?

The Great Gatsby
By F. Scott Fitzgerald

SWIFTSNOTES

Not fresh on *The Great Gatsby*? Don't worry! Here's a quick rundown:

✶ Nick Carraway, the story's narrator, moves to West Egg, right next door to Jay Gatsby, a charismatic yet mysterious man who's famous for throwing over-the-top parties.

✶ Gatsby is head over heels for his former love Daisy Buchanan, Nick's cousin, who is living the fancy, upper class life in East Egg with her less-than-charming husband, Tom.

✶ With Nick's help, Gatsby and Daisy start to rekindle their old flame – despite the minor issue of Daisy being, you know, still married to Tom.

✶ Tom notices, and he isn't thrilled, which is hypocritical considering he has a lover too. He confronts Gatsby in a dramatic showdown.

✶ Daisy storms off and, while driving Gatsby's car, accidentally hits Tom's mistress, Myrtle. But *gasp* ... Gatsby takes the blame!

✶ Myrtle's heartbroken husband gets revenge by killing Gatsby, then himself. Nick, who is *so* over the drama by this point, moves back to the Midwest.

THE GREAT GATSBY
&
Dear Reader

Maybe it's her larger-than-life concerts or her fascination with daisies, but there is more than one invisible string tying Taylor Swift to *The Great Gatsby*. "This Is Why We Can't Have Nice Things" channels a champagne-fuelled sense of grandeur, while "happiness" nods to Daisy 's famous quote about being a "beautiful little fool".

And yet, "Dear Reader" gives us arguably the strongest tie to *The Great Gatsby* through its exploration of perspective. Taylor often shifts perspectives in her music – such as writing from a man's POV in "betty" – and even admits to lying to us in "I Can Do It With a Broken Heart". But in "Dear Reader", her lyrics are layered with contradictions. She guides listeners into trusting her, all while hinting that there's probably another side to the story we're not seeing. These are classic traits of an unreliable narrator.

TAYLOR SWIFT VS. NICK CARRAWAY

Just like Nick Carraway in *The Great Gatsby*, Taylor becomes an unreliable narrator in "Dear Reader" by contradicting herself, blurring illusion and reality, and keeping secrets.

CONTRADICTING HERSELF

In "Dear Reader", Taylor repeatedly warns us not to listen to someone who is falling apart. With her first-person lyrics describing insomnia, pacing, drinking too much and crying out for help, she creates a deeply personal narrative. Because Taylor has described *Midnights* (the album that includes "Dear Reader") as a collection inspired by sleepless nights throughout her life, it's easy to assume she's talking about herself in the song. And let's be honest, you probably wouldn't take advice from someone feeling like this! However, later in the song, she offers advice anyway, but it's to find someone else to follow. This sends mixed signals and contradicts her earlier message, making her an unreliable narrator.

Nick Carraway opens *The Great Gatsby* by telling us his father taught him not to judge others. Yet, not long after, he contradicts himself by judging Tom Buchanan for having "two shining, arrogant eyes" – the first of many judgements Nick makes about the East Egg elites. Like Taylor, Nick's contradictions show he is an unreliable narrator. Both "characters" keep us questioning the story they're telling.

✶ Where else does Taylor contradict herself in her songs? Do these contradictions impact how much you trust her as a storyteller?

BLURRING ILLUSION & REALITY

Check out the first verse of "Dear Reader" – Taylor floats this grand idea of burning the evidence of your past so that you become unrecognizable even to yourself. She's talking about running away from reality and toward illusion. This is classic avoidant-attachment behaviour – choosing the comfort of a false, safe space rather than facing reality head-on.

Similarly, in *The Great Gatsby*, Nick tells us he is one of the only honest people he has ever known. But his actions constantly tell a different story, such as when he omits the truth by not telling Tom Buchanan about Daisy and Gatsby's affair. Nick is actually so good at lying that he convinces himself that he always tells the truth. He builds up an illusion of honesty that's far from the reality he's living in.

KEEPING SECRETS

Taylor knows just how valuable a secret is, and she won't let you forget it! In "Dear Reader", she talks about the power and luxury of keeping things to yourself. Hiding things from your audience is a typical move for an unreliable narrator.

Nick Carraway, with his fascination for Gatsby and the glitzy life he's built, also holds details back from readers – whether he means to or not. His loyalty to Gatsby stops him from talking about his friend's dark past … about how Gatsby's wealth is tied to shady business deals and organized crime, and he is connected to a man named Meyer Wolfsheim who supposedly fixed the World Series. Despite knowing these red flags, Nick focuses on Gatsby's charm and his big dreams, which leaves us to figure out the truth about him.

Taylor and Nick remind us that what is left unsaid is just as important as what they reveal, leaving us to question how much of the story we're really being told.

✶ **In "Dear Reader", what do you think Taylor might be keeping secret?**

THE UNRELIABLE NARRATOR & *Blank Space*

"Blank Space" is a fan-favourite for a reason. The *1989* single was one of the first songs Taylor used to fire back at critics who called her "boy-crazy".

In the song's second verse, she basically calls herself a trainwreck you can't look away from. By describing herself as chaos disguised as a good time, she flips her haters' words into something so catchy you can't help but love it. Instead of getting defensive, she leaned into the image, exaggerated it and used the song to take back control of the narrative.

By manipulating this story to her advantage, she shows up as the ultimate unreliable narrator.

The "Blank Space" music video does an excellent job of casting Taylor as an unreliable storyteller. It swings between the extremes of Taylor as the ideal, glamorous partner and her as a jealous, vengeful lover.

The video exaggerates these personalities so much that you wonder if, alongside the humour, Taylor's real feelings are on show here too. The dramatic moments – such as stabbing a cake and throwing a phone into a fountain – keep us questioning whether she is actually this angry or if she is just making fun of the way the media has painted her.

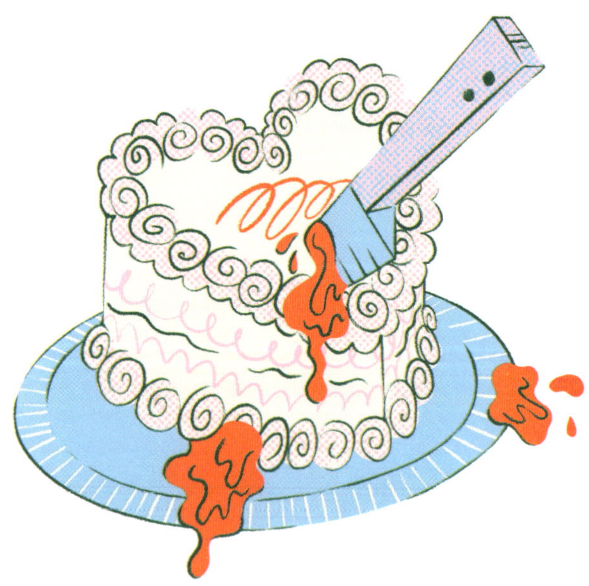

✶ List your top three over-the-top lyrics or music video moments from "Blank Space" where Taylor exaggerates her own image.

Think about these questions to explore the topic further.

∗ In which other songs does Taylor show up as an unreliable narrator?

✶ In songs such as "tolerate it", Taylor sings about the pain of neglect, which led to her manipulation, and alters her perspective of the situation she's in. Does this make her an unreliable narrator?

✶ If you could shift the perspective in one of Taylor's songs to make the narrator fully reliable, which song would you choose? How might the song differ if the narrator were entirely honest?

CHAPTER 2

A Modern-Day Romantic Poet

Discovering Romanticism in Taylor Swift's music

THE BOOKSHELF

Romeo and Juliet
Wuthering Heights

THE PLAYLIST

"Love Story"
"Enchanted"
"Paris"
"ivy"
"the lakes"

Queue up this chapter's songs to listen and follow along!

Discovering Romanticism

When we say "romantic", we don't necessarily mean making grand gestures like proposing on one knee on a bed of rose petals.

Romanticism was a movement in the late 18th century that influenced all forms of art – painting, music, theatre and literature. It was all about emotion, imagination, individuality and pushing back against the strict rules of the Enlightenment – a 17th-century movement known for reason, science and logic.

Romantic artists loved to highlight the beauty and power of nature, sometimes with a mysterious or supernatural twist. In literature, this meant authors focused on personal feelings, the wonders of the world and exploring the unknown. Whether through art, music or writing, the goal was to capture raw human emotion and the awe-inspiring forces of nature.

Romanticism also pushed back against traditional society and questioned its rules and values. It celebrated being different and free!

To understand Taylor's music and lyrics it helps to understand Romanticism. This chapter looks at how Taylor Swift's songs such as "Love Story", "Enchanted", "Paris", "ivy" and "the lakes" reflect common Romantic themes from popular stories including *Romeo and Juliet* and *Wuthering Heights*. We'll look at how Taylor uses Romantic elements in her music, and you'll learn how to find the Romantic Easter eggs Taylor has hidden in each song.

Let's begin with a few questions to focus your mind.

* What immediately comes to mind when you hear the word "romantic"?

✶ **Do you think there's a difference between a love story and a Romantic one? Why?**

✶ **Some people dismiss Taylor Swift's work as "silly love songs". Do you think songs such as "Love Story", "Enchanted", "Paris", "ivy" and "the lakes" fall into that category? Or do they carry more depth and meaning than they're often given credit for?**

FROM SHAKESPEARE TO SWIFT

Although William Shakespeare's work predates the Romantic movement by, give or take, 300 years, his works are undeniably Romantic. The Bard had an unmatched ability to explore the boundaries of human experience through his writing.

There is a reason why he is still considered one of the greatest writers today. His work has been referenced in modern artwork of all kinds, from Broadway to the big screen. Taylor Swift alludes to Shakespearian tragedies *Romeo and Juliet*, *Macbeth* and *Hamlet*, and the comedy *All's Well That Ends Well*, in her music.

✶ Can you name any Taylor songs or music videos that reference Shakespeare's famous works?

Romeo and Juliet

By William Shakespeare

SWIFTSNOTES

If you didn't cover *Romeo and Juliet* in your literature class, or maybe it's been a while, here is a quick refresher:

✶ Romeo Montague and Juliet Capulet fall head over heels in love at a masked ball, despite their families hating each other's guts.

✶ They sneak off to get married, with Friar Laurence's help, hopeful that their decision will end the feud between their families.

✶ Juliet's cousin, Tybalt, kills Mercutio, Romeo's close friend. In a bold move to avenge Mercutio's death, Romeo kills Tybalt – and ends up banished for it.

✶ Friar Laurence comes up with a plan for Juliet to fake her death and run away with Romeo, but when Romeo finds her, he believes she is actually dead, so he drinks poison.

✶ Juliet wakes up, sees Romeo has died, and decides to join him by taking her own life.

✶ After their tragic end, the Montagues and Capulets realise they've been acting like idiots and end their feud.

ROMEO AND JULIET
&
Love Story

"Love Story" name-drops Romeo and Juliet throughout the song and uses their story as a metaphor for a sweeping, dramatic romance. Beyond the direct mentions, you'll also find plenty of Romantic themes akin to Shakespeare's great tragedy.

"But, soft! What light through yonder window breaks?
It is the east, and Juliet is the sun!"

Shakespeare's famous line from Act II of *Romeo and Juliet* paints Juliet in an almost holy light. It perfectly captures Romeo's love-stricken teenage reaction to seeing her on her private balcony.

"Love Story" idealizes love in a similar way and portrays it as a *Romeo and Juliet*-like fairy tale. Taylor's retelling of the story is so optimistic that her version of the story ends with a hopeful twist that differs from the original. She leans into the belief that love conquers all.

✶ Songs such as "Love Story" and stories such as *Romeo and Juliet* depict idealized and dramatic versions of love. What do you think these portrayals get right about love, and where might they fall short? What lyrics or moments support your thinking?

INDIVIDUALISM

"Love Story" captures personal emotions, such as Juliet's restlessness to be with her Romeo, and the struggles, including her fight with her father, to make it happen. This focus on individual feelings over societal expectations is common within Romanticism.

✶ Which lyrics in "Love Story" reflect the rollercoaster of emotions our narrator is going though?

NATURE IMAGERY

The song hints at escaping to a natural place for love – such as a beautiful garden balcony – mirroring the iconic scenes in *Romeo and Juliet*. It fits with the Romantic idea that nature is the best setting in which to feel deep emotions.

✶ Which settings are mentioned in "Love Story"? How many of these are outside in nature?

ROMEO AND JULIET
&
Enchanted

What do you think of this quote from Act I of *Romeo and Juliet*?

"Did my heart love till now? Forswear it, sight!
For I ne'er saw true beauty till this night."

This is the moment Romeo first lays eyes on Juliet at the masquerade ball.

It sounds pretty similar to the mesmerizing first encounter Taylor describes in "Enchanted", don't you think? The song captures the magic and intensity of feeling an instant connection with someone.

✶ Which lyrics from "Enchanted" have the same "Sparks Fly" energy as Romeo's first sight of Juliet?

THE POWER OF NIGHT

In *Romeo and Juliet*, and in many of Shakespeare's works, the night is a time of magic, transformation and intimacy. For the star-crossed lovers, it's a time when they can be together, away from the conflicts of their feuding families and social obligations.

In a similar way, "Enchanted" captures the magic of a "sparkling" night and how that can help to build a deep connection with someone.

✶ How does the setting in "Enchanted" make the moment the narrator is experiencing feel special? Which lyrics stand out to you that show this connection?

Wuthering Heights
By Emily Brontë

SWIFTSNOTES

Not familiar with this Brontë classic? Here's an overview of *Wuthering Heights*:

✶ Mr Earnshaw takes in Heathcliff, a mysterious and dirty orphan who forms a complicated bond with Earnshaw's daughter, Catherine. Heathcliff and Catherine fall in love – their relationship is tied to the freedom and wildness of the local moors.

✶ After Earnshaw dies, Heathcliff is mistreated by Catherine's brother, Hindley, who makes him a servant at their home, Wuthering Heights.

✶ Catherine, who lives for the drama, marries Edgar Linton for his social status, which leaves Heathcliff with a broken heart and a burning desire for revenge against the Linton siblings.

✶ Heathcliff disappears for three years and returns educated and wealthy. He marries Edgar's sister, Isabella, just to get under Catherine's skin.

✶ Catherine dies after giving birth to Edgar's daughter, Cathy, which sends Heathcliff into a deeper spiral of heartbreak and vengeance against Edgar, Hindley and anyone else he thinks is responsible for his pain.

✶ Heathcliff eventually takes over Wuthering Heights and the Lintons' estates, but his obsession with Catherine haunts him until his last breath. The story ends with Cathy and Hareton (Hindley's son) planning to marry. (Yes, they are cousins).

WUTHERING HEIGHTS
&
Paris

When Heathcliff is overwhelmed with love and despair after Catherine's death, Paris calls out, "I *cannot* live without my life! I *cannot* live without my soul!"

We see this same kind of intensity, emotion and idealization of love mirrored in Taylor Swift's song "Paris". It's a bit lighter, sure, but look at the song's chorus, where she talks about her love being so strong that it affects her breathing!

The powerful love described in "Paris" mirrors the intense, stormy relationship between Heathcliff and Catherine on the isolated Yorkshire moors. Just like our main characters from *Wuthering Heights*, the lovers in "Paris" totally isolate themselves, avoiding reality, brushing off gossip and ignoring the news to focus entirely on each other.

THE POWER OF PLACE AND IMAGINATION

Just as the wild, untamed moors in *Wuthering Heights* represent freedom and the passion between Heathcliff and Catherine, Taylor Swift uses the city of Paris in her song as a dreamy escape for her lovers. Paris becomes a metaphorical place that feels magical, and it symbolizes how love can bring beauty and meaning to their lives.

✶ Where else in Taylor's music does a setting – like Paris or the moors – give the story more depth?

WUTHERING HEIGHTS
&
ivy

In "ivy", Taylor's repeated metaphor of being "covered" by someone you love hints at a deep, all-consuming connection. This brings us right back to the moors in *Wuthering Heights* and how the untamed land symbolizes Heathcliff and Catherine's uncontrollable love.

Both “ivy” and *Wuthering Heights* use nature to illustrate the power of love. In *Wuthering Heights*, the moors represent a love that is wild and free, while in “ivy”, the plant signifies a love that grows and entangles everything around it.

*** How does the metaphor of ivy in Taylor Swift’s song reflect the kind of love being described? Which lyrics support your thoughts?**

the lakes

The song "the lakes" is Taylor's most blatant nod to Romanticism, and there's a reason for that.

THE OPENING LINE SETS THE TONE

She immediately starts reflecting!

✶ **Write down the first line of "the lakes":**

✶ **What emotions or thoughts does it bring up for you?**

A FASCINATION WITH MORTALITY

Taylor starts singing about elegies, which are mournful poems written for the dead. This goes hand-in-hand with the Romantic idea that there's beauty in remembering those we've lost.

∗ Why do you think themes of life and death are so important in Romanticism?

ESCAPING THE CHAOS OF MODERN LIFE

In this song, Taylor dreams of a world far from "hunters", or the paparazzi, and the noise of social media.

∗ What does Taylor's desire to escape say about the pressures of fame and modern life?

LOVE FOR NATURE

Romantic works of art love to celebrate the beauty of nature – especially in places like Windermere in the English Lake District, a place known as inspiration for poets such as William Wordsworth, the father of Romantic poetry.

✶ Write down your favourite nature-inspired lyric from "the lakes".

✶ Why would Taylor use nature as the setting for her escape?

A CLEVER REFERENCE

Speaking of Wordsworth, did you catch his name? Taylor sneaks in a reference to William Wordsworth in the song's second verse.

✶ Write down the lyric that hints at Wordsworth.

✶ What effect does name-dropping him in such a playful, ironic way have on the song?

✶ What other elements of Romanticism show up in "the lakes"?

Think about these questions to explore the topic further.

* What other Taylor Swift songs remind you of the Romantic ideas in *Romeo and Juliet* and *Wuthering Heights*?

✶ When Taylor Swift started writing songs, do you think she meant to include themes from Romantic literary works, or did it just happen?

✶ How has Taylor's music changed over time to show that she might be including these themes and stories on purpose?

✶ Think of other Romantic stories you know. If Taylor wrote a song inspired by one of them, what themes or details do you think she would focus on to make it her own?

CHAPTER 3
Growing Up & Getting Old

The coming-of-age theme found in Taylor Swift's music

THE BOOKSHELF	THE PLAYLIST
Peter and Wendy	"Peter"
To Kill a Mockingbird	"seven"
	"The Best Day"

Queue up this chapter's songs to listen and follow along!

Coming-of-Age Stories

The coming-of-age trope in storytelling and literature is a theme that focuses on the growth and development of a character, usually from childhood or adolescence into adulthood.

Stories with this theme explore the challenges, experiences and lessons that shape a character's identity and understanding of the world. In simple terms, coming of age is about growing up and finding yourself.

Coming-of-age stories can be traced back to the 18th-century German *bildungsroman*, which means "formation novel". A *bildungsroman* is a detailed journey of one character's personal, moral and psychological growth, while a coming-of-age story is one about growing up, even if it only focuses on a specific moment in time, or one event in that process.

While all *bildungsroman* are coming-of-age stories, not all coming-of-age stories are *bildungsroman*.

THE ANATOMY OF A COMING-OF-AGE STORY

Here are the key elements to keep an eye out for in this genre:

✶ **Character development:**
The main character grows and learns important lessons that help them understand themselves and the world better.

✶ **Facing challenges:**
The character faces problems that test their strength and beliefs, such as personal issues, family problems or pressure from their peers.

✶ **Self-discovery:**
The character goes on a journey to find out who they are, what they believe and what they want in life.

✶ **Maturity:**
By the end of the story, the character has matured, and has a better sense of themselves and the direction they want their life to go in.

To understand Taylor's music and lyrics, it's useful to understand the coming-of-age story. This chapter looks at how Taylor Swift's songs, such as "Peter", "seven" and "The Best Day", reflect common coming-of-age themes from popular stories such as *Peter and Wendy* and *To Kill a Mockingbird*. We'll see how Taylor uses these themes in her music, and you'll learn how to find the coming-of-age Easter eggs she has hidden in each song.

Let's begin with a few questions to focus your mind.

⁎ If you could go back to any age from your childhood, which age would you choose and why? What made that time special to you?

✶ Do you think a coming-of-age story is most authentic when it's written by a young person as they are experiencing it, or by an adult reflecting on their past?

✶ Which Taylor Swift song about growing up do you most relate to, and why?

Peter and Wendy
By J. M. Barrie

SWIFTSNOTES

Whether you know Disney's *Peter Pan* best or prefer J. M. Barrie's adventure novel from 1911, here is a quick rundown of the story of *Peter and Wendy*:

✶ Wendy, John and Michael Darling live in London with their parents and their dog, Nana.

✶ One night, Peter Pan flies into their nursery with his fairy sidekick, Tinker Bell, and teaches the children how to fly.

✶ They travel to Neverland, a magical island home to a group named the Lost Boys, mermaids, pirates and the story's villain: Captain Hook.

✶ In Neverland, Wendy acts like a mother figure to Peter and the Lost Boys by telling them stories and treating them like a family.

✶ Their adventure in Neverland peaks when Peter Pan and Captain Hook face off in an epic battle that ends when Hook meets his fate – getting swallowed by a crocodile!

✶ Peter Pan stays in Neverland, but the Darling children return home to their parents. Wendy grows up, and years later, her daughter Jane takes her place, carrying on the adventures with Peter, who remains a child forever.

PETER AND WENDY
&
Peter

In case the name of the song wasn't enough of a clue, Taylor Swift's "Peter" is a direct reference to the story *Peter and Wendy*.

Beyond references to lost boys and never growing up (cue the song from the *Speak Now* album), the song explores themes of:

* **Broken promises**
* **Preserving childhood**
* **Disappointment in reality**

BROKEN PROMISES

The lyrics of "Peter" feel like the kind of promises kids make to each other – pledges that are full of hope at the time, but that don't hold up as time passes. The song captures the heartbreak of waiting for a connection that never comes, as the realities of growing up make those agreements impossible to keep. This tension – the pull between holding on to those promises and facing reality – is reflected in the story of *Peter and Wendy*, as Peter wants to stay a kid forever, but Wendy chooses to grow up and move forward.

∗ **What stands out to you about the repeated lyrics in the chorus of "Peter"?**

PRESERVING CHILDHOOD

Both "Peter" and *Peter and Wendy* tell their stories with a sense of nostalgia. In her song, Taylor expresses a longing for the past, a desire to hold onto her childhood memories, and we get the sense that she is yearning to preserve her innocence and joy.

In a similar way, Mrs Darling cares for her children by "tidying up their minds", her nightly ritual of removing their bad thoughts after they fall asleep. In "Peter", the preservation of childhood is rooted in the narrator's longing to retain her memories. She holds on to as much as she can, even though life has made it impossible to keep the memories fully intact. In *Peter and Wendy*, this preservation is seen through Mrs Darling's actions. Both stories emphasize the importance of holding on to your childhood for as long as possible.

DISAPPOINTMENT IN REALITY

In "Peter", Taylor uses the bridge of the song to express both the hope she once had and her disappointment when she realised her childhood dreams wouldn't come true.

Similarly, in *Peter and Wendy*, Barrie's famous opening line, "All children, except one, grow up", immediately introduces readers to the reality of having to leave your childhood behind – it happens to all of us, whether we want it to or not.

✶ Imagine you're sitting with Wendy from *Peter and Wendy* and Taylor (or the narrator of the song "Peter"). They're talking about childhood promises that didn't come true. How do the lyrics in "Peter" connect to this reality of growing up that many of us experience?

✶ Do you relate more to the song, the book or both in how they capture the bittersweet side of growing up?

To Kill a Mockingbird
By Harper Lee

SWIFTSNOTES

***To Kill a Mockingbird* is a classic, but if you're not familiar with it, no worries! Here is a quick crash course:**

* Scout Finch, her brother Jem and their friend Dill are determined to get their antisocial neighbour, Boo Radley, out of his house.

* Scout and Jem's father, the lawyer Atticus Finch, is appointed to defend Tom Robinson, a Black man accused of raping Mayella Ewell, a white woman.

* During the trial, it becomes clear that Tom is innocent and that Mayella and her father, Bob Ewell, are lying, but the all-white jury convicts Tom anyway.

* After the trial, Bob Ewell seeks revenge on Atticus and his children. He attacks Scout and Jem on their way home from a Halloween party, but Boo Radley steps in and saves them.

* Boo Radley ends up killing Bob Ewell in defence of the children, but the sheriff decides to cover up the truth to protect Boo, who is a shy and usually gentle man.

* Scout reflects on the lessons she has learned about empathy, compassion and the complexities of human nature, as she stands on Boo Radley's porch looking out at her neighbourhood.

TO KILL A MOCKINGBIRD & *seven*

The song "seven" captures the simplicity of childhood friendships, just like the bond between Scout, Jem and Dill in *To Kill a Mockingbird*.

The song and the book both celebrate the pure joy of being a child before adult problems get in the way. The carefree days of playing together, imagining different worlds and building those first meaningful connections with others are at the heart of both stories.

✝ Does the friendship Taylor describes in "seven" remind you of any of your own childhood friendships?

COMING-OF-AGE MEETS LOSS-OF-INNOCENCE

Looking at the coming-of-age theme in *To Kill a Mockingbird* and Taylor Swift's "seven", we can see how both stories explore the loss of innocence. In "seven", there's a longing for the carefree days of childhood – swinging over trees and spending summer with friends – before the struggles with home life and growing up take hold.

Similarly, in the novel, readers see Scout and Jem's innocence break after they experience the injustice of Tom Robinson's trial. When Jem says, "It's like bein' a caterpillar in a cocoon ... I always thought Maycomb folks were the best folks in the world, least that's what they seemed like," reflects the moment they begin to understand just how unfair the world can be.

Both the song and the book capture that shift from being a child to facing the tough realities of life.

✶ Which lyrics in "seven" reflect the mixed emotions of looking back on childhood?

SAFE IN OUR OWN LITTLE WORLD

Taylor's song "seven" also shows how kids look out for each other, just like Scout, Jem and Dill do in *To Kill a Mockingbird*. In the song, they create their own little world to escape from an angry father and a home where they feel like they have to hide who they are. These moments in the song remind us of how the children in the book stick together and find comfort in their friendship as they start to see how complicated the world is.

✶ If you could create a world to escape to like the one in "seven", what would it look like?

TO KILL A MOCKINGBIRD
&
The Best Day

"The Best Day" might just be the sweetest song about a mother-daughter relationship ever written. This *Fearless*-era classic showcases some of Taylor's favourite memories with her mother, Andrea, through lyrics and the nostalgic home footage featured in the music video.

The "The Best Day" music video Muse captures the simple, heartfelt moments that define Taylor's bond with her mother, including watching fireworks and reading together in their pyjamas. These moments are a lot like the everyday moments Scout shares with her father in *To Kill a Mockingbird*, such as when they read together on the porch. Both relationships are full of love, support and understanding, grounded in the small but meaningful experiences that shape who we become.

✶ Are there any lyrics from "The Best Day" that make you think of the relationship between Scout and her father Atticus?

Taylor Talkback

Think about these questions to explore the topic further.

✶ Would you label any of the songs discussed in this lesson as *bildungsroman*? If so, why? What about any of Taylor's other songs?

✶ Could you argue that all of Taylor's songs are coming-of-age themed, since they touch on the four key parts of a coming-of-age story (character development, facing challenges, self-discovery and maturity)?

✶ Should young people be exposed to the mature themes in songs such as Taylor Swift's "seven" and stories such as *To Kill a Mockingbird*, or are those more suitable for adults?

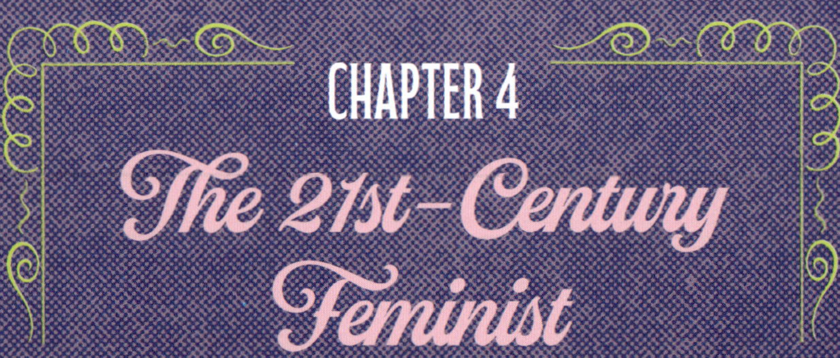

CHAPTER 4

The 21st-Century Feminist

The exploration of feminine identity in Taylor Swift's music

THE BOOKSHELF

The Bell Jar
Jane Eyre

THE PLAYLIST

"The Man"
"mad woman"
"Miss Americana & The Heartbreak Prince"
""""Slut!""""

Queue up this chapter's songs to listen and follow along!

Exploring Feminism

Feminism is a movement that has changed and grown over time. It is shaped by the needs of each generation.

In the 21st century, feminism takes many different forms. It's intersectional; it's sexually diverse; it's contemporary; *and* it's rooted in history.

Some of the greatest female authors in history challenged the norms of their time, each in their own way, and helped shape what feminism means today.

Jane Austen created strong and intelligent female protagonists who asserted their right to choose love or independence over financial security.

Toni Morrison illuminated the lives of Black women, their resilience and their determination to define themselves despite the weight of history and oppression.

Virginia Woolf advocated for women's intellectual freedom and their right to create and write freely in a "room of [their] own".

Louisa May Alcott wrote about women who prioritized their ambitions over following traditional gender roles.

These authors, along with many before and after them, used literature to empower women by telling stories of resistance and agency, where women stand up against oppression and make their own choices. These stories give a voice to women's experiences, thoughts and emotions, and highlight the power of sisterhood and the support women can offer each other.

"Feminism is probably the most important movement that you could embrace, because it's just basically another word for equality."

Taylor Swift for *Maxim*, 2015

While she hasn't written her support for women into a novel (yet), Taylor Swift carries the legacy of this movement into the 21st century through her music.

To understand Taylor's music and lyrics, it helps to understand the feminist literary movement. This chapter looks at how Taylor Swift's songs such as "The Man", "mad woman", "Miss Americana & The Heartbreak Prince" and ""Slut!"" reflect common feminist themes from popular stories such as *The Bell Jar* and *Jane Eyre*. We'll see how Taylor writes these themes into her music, and you'll learn how to find the feminist Easter eggs Taylor has hidden in each song.

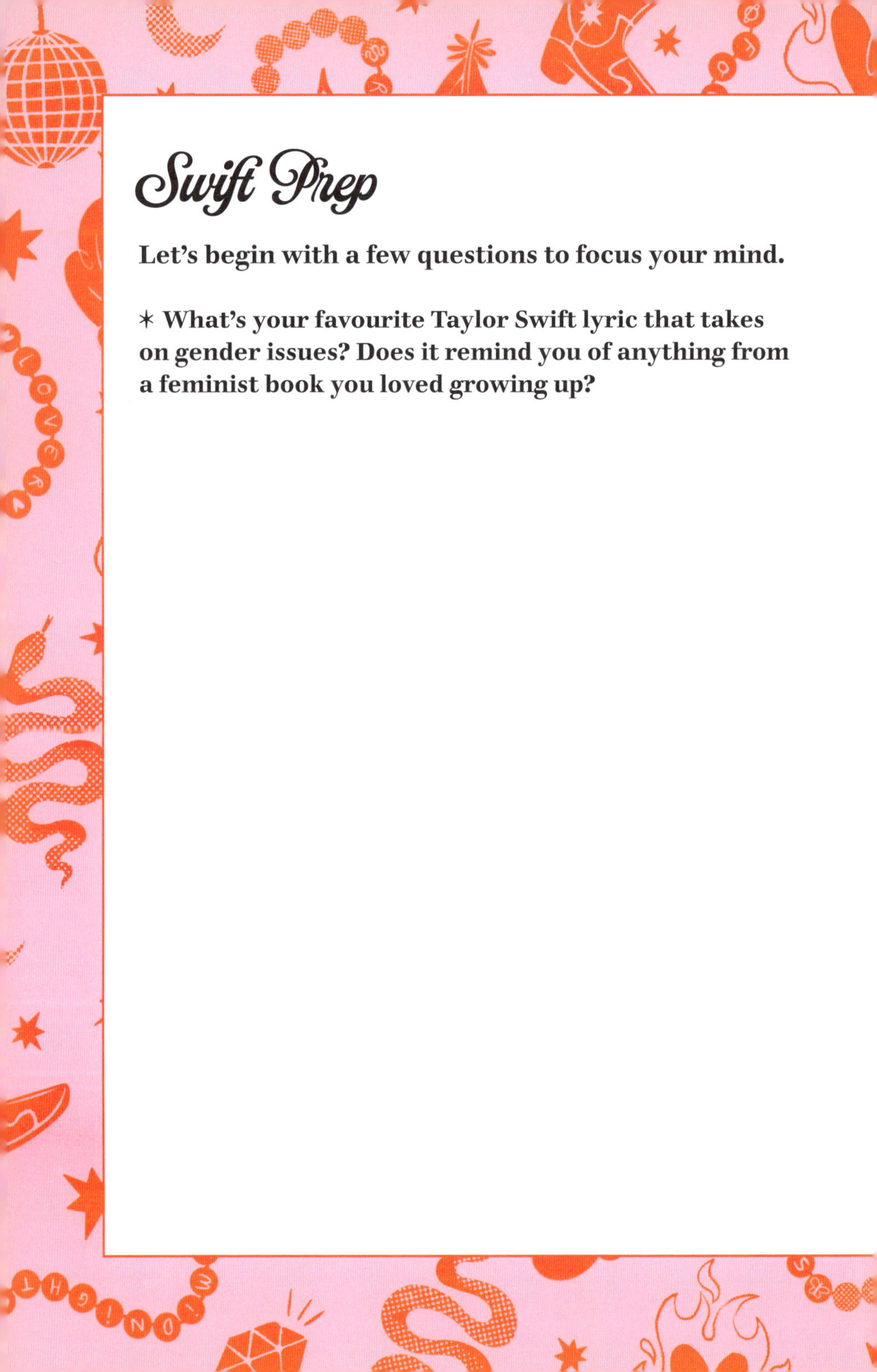

Swift Prep

Let's begin with a few questions to focus your mind.

∗ What's your favourite Taylor Swift lyric that takes on gender issues? Does it remind you of anything from a feminist book you loved growing up?

✶ Why do you think female anger is often perceived differently than male anger, both in art and in life?

✶ How have feminist stories evolved over time, from the eras of *The Bell Jar* and *Jane Eyre* to the ever-changing eras of Taylor Swift's music?

I AM
I AM
I AM
The Bell Jar
By Sylvia Plath
I AM
I AM
I AM

SWIFTSNOTES

Whether you know her as Sylvia Plath, or by her pseudonym Victoria Lucas, her only published novel, *The Bell Jar*, remains a defining work of 20th-century literature. Here's a quick overview:

✶ Esther Greenwood, a talented young woman, wins an internship at a prestigious magazine in New York City. She struggles with her mental health, feeling out of place in the competitive, glamorous environment and overwhelmed by the pressure to meet the expectations of others.

✶ After returning home to Boston, Esther's depression worsens and leaves her feeling trapped by the 1950s expectations of being the perfect woman. Despondent and lost, she struggles to write or find direction in her life.

✶ She tries different treatments for her depression, but nothing works. Her mental state deteriorates, and she ends up hospitalized after a suicide attempt.

✶ Esther goes through electroconvulsive therapy at the psychiatric hospital and begins to confront her inner demons.

✶ Through the support of her doctor and her own stubborn resilience, she starts to bounce back, slowly but surely reclaiming control over her life.

✶ Esther prepares to leave the hospital with an uncertain future ahead of her, but also a newfound strength and a better understanding of herself.

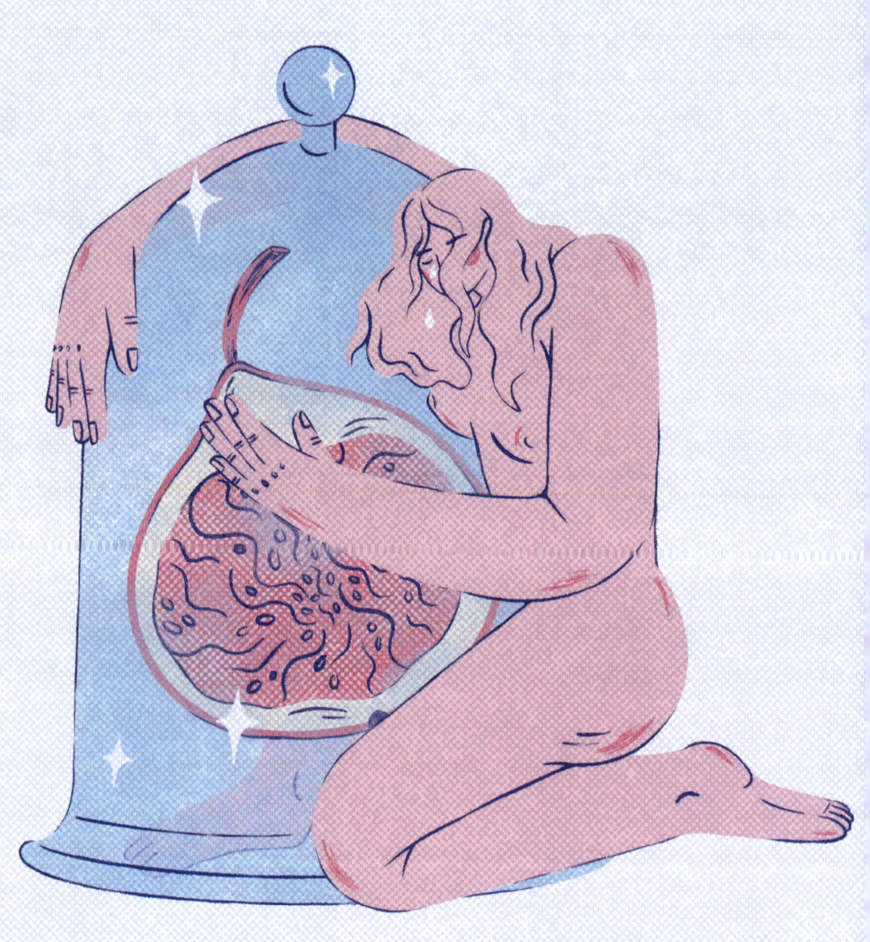

THE BELL JAR & *The Man*

Esther Greenwood faces the same kind of frustrations that Taylor Swift's "The Man" puts into straightforward – and catchy – lyrics about the double standards women face.

Like Taylor, Esther is stuck in a world where her every move is judged or limited because of society's expectations.

Plath describes this perfectly with her iconic fig tree metaphor from *The Bell Jar*. She imagines her life as a sprawling tree, with each branch offering a fat, ripe fig – one fig is marriage and children, another is becoming a famous poet, another is a successful career and so on. But as she sits there, unable to pick just one, the figs slowly start to shrivel, blacken and drop to the ground. It's a brutally honest portrayal of how the paralysis of indecision doesn't just keep you stuck – it strips you of every option until there's nothing left but regret.

The metaphor of the fig tree perfectly captures Esther's frustration with the limited choices women had and her fear that society's expectations would hold her back – similar to the ideas that Taylor calls out in "The Man". In the chorus, Taylor sings about how men are praised for things women get judged for and paints a picture of how much easier life would be if she were a man. It's a powerful way to show just how frustrating it is to deal with these inequalities.

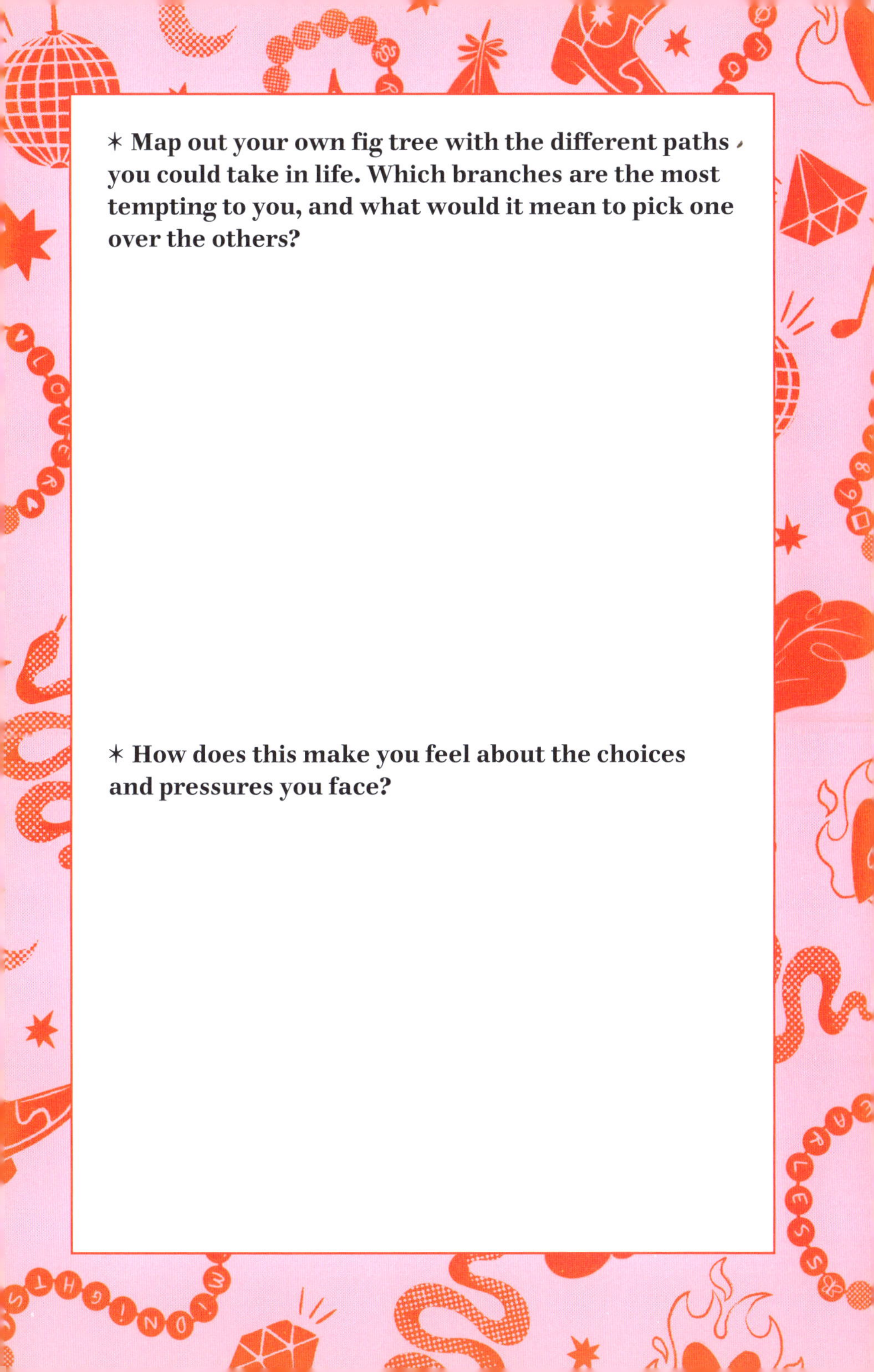

✶ Map out your own fig tree with the different paths you could take in life. Which branches are the most tempting to you, and what would it mean to pick one over the others?

✶ How does this make you feel about the choices and pressures you face?

THE BELL JAR
&
mad woman

Both *The Bell Jar* and "mad woman" take a sharp jab at the unfair expectations placed on women.

In the novel, Esther's frustration boils over as she realises she "[can't] stand the idea of a woman having to have a single pure life and a man being able to have a double life, one pure and one not". This unfairness eats away at her, fuelling her anger and mistrust toward these expectations.

In "mad woman", Taylor Swift channels that same sense of anger. The scorpion metaphor in the song – it stings when provoked – captures the urge to fight back when you've been pushed too far.

✶ Taylor's scorpion visual in "mad woman" is fierce – and spot on. If you were to rewrite this part of the song, what other imagery or metaphors could you use to express that same "enough is enough" moment?

Jane Eyre

By Charlotte Brontë

SWIFTSNOTES

It's another Brontë sister's time to shine! If you're not familiar with *Jane Eyre*, that's okay, here is a crash course on this 19th-century classic:

✶ Jane Eyre has a tough childhood, first living at her aunt's house and later at a strict boarding school called Lowood Institution.

✶ Despite her challenges at boarding school, Jane excels academically and eventually becomes a teacher at Lowood.

✶ She wants more independence, so Jane takes a governess job at Thornfield Hall, where she meets and falls in love with the mysterious Mr Rochester.

✶ Just as the relationship gets serious, Jane discovers Mr Rochester is already married to another woman, Bertha Mason, and that she has been living in the attic of Thornfield Hall. Reasonably freaked out, Jane leaves.

✶ Jane loses all her money and has a rough time on her own, but eventually she rests with the Rivers family, who turn out to be her cousins. She also conveniently inherits a large fortune from a long-lost relative.

✶ Bertha sets Thornfield Hall on fire and dies in the blaze, and Jane reunites with Mr Rochester after hearing him calling to her. He is now blind and apologetic. They marry, and Jane finds happiness, balancing independence with love.

The Man.

JANE EYRE & *The Man*

The eldest Brontë sister, like her younger siblings, had to publish her brilliant works under a pseudonym. And not just any pseudonym – she had to use a man's name, Currer Bell. Back then, women's writing didn't get the respect it deserved, and many topics were off-limits for them to discuss.

This includes the very topics discussed in *Jane Eyre*: female independence, social class and mental health.

✶ What are some topics you'd love to see more women writing about?

While Taylor didn't write "The Man" under a fake name, she did dress up like a man for the song's music video to make the point that there are double standards for men and women.

The video for "The Man" critiques how society lets men get away with all kinds of nonsense – manspreading, being sore losers at sports and using their kids to get attention from women, to name just a few.

If Taylor Swift faces this kind of inequity today, imagine how tough it was for the Bronte sisters. They had to use male pseudonyms in the 19th century because they knew their work would be dismissed if readers knew they were women.

✶ If the Brontë sisters were alive today, what kinds of stories or topics do you think they would write about?

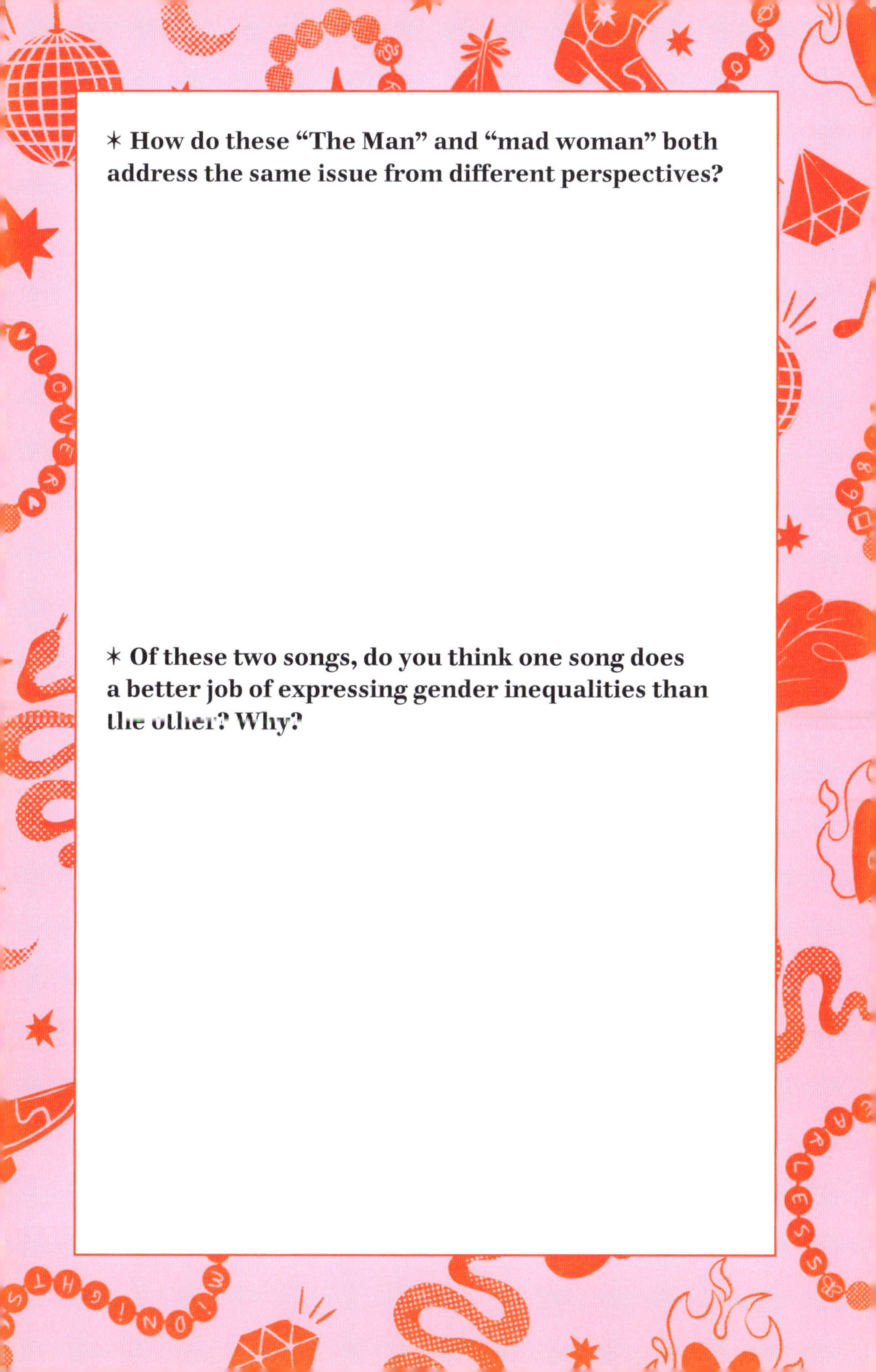

✶ How do these "The Man" and "mad woman" both address the same issue from different perspectives?

✶ Of these two songs, do you think one song does a better job of expressing gender inequalities than the other? Why?

miss AMERiCANA

Miss Americana & The Heartbreak Prince

Taylor's iconic Eras Tour opener, "Miss Americana & The Heartbreak Prince", might not scream "feminist anthem" at first listen, but once you start paying attention to the lyrics, the themes will jump out.

Let's break down how this song connects to the five key points of feminist writing.

FLIPPING THE SCRIPT ON GENDER ROLES

Notice how the song leans into the "bad girl" label. Instead of letting it be a put-down, the lyrics turn it into a badge of honour!

A classic moment in any feminist text is when a character pushes back against gender roles.

Just like those fierce heroines, this song says, "Yeah, I'm a bad girl. What of it?"

CALLING OUT THE PATRIARCHY

Pay attention to the song's metaphor about rolling dice and playing games.

This isn't just clever wordplay – it's a not-so-subtle critique of how the game (of life) can be pretty unfair, especially for women. The idea ties into how society expects people – again, mainly women – to play along with its rules, even when the rewards are meaningless, or the odds are stacked against them. The song highlights how trying to succeed in a system built on judgement and superficial expectations feels like a losing battle.

Feminist works love to call out these unfair systems, and this song is no exception, throwing shade at the way the patriarchy stacks the deck.

POWER IN NUMBERS

✶ **What do you notice about the bond between Miss Americana and the Heartbreak Prince?**

Feminist literature loves to highlight the power of relationships where people lift each other up, and this song does just that by making it clear that the title characters have each other's backs.

It's more than just a romantic connection; it's a declaration of solidarity!

SURVIVING THE BATTLEFIELD

The imagery of being worn down while standing up to the bad guys in the song's fourth verse is vivid.

Characters fight through hostile environments all the time in feminist literature, and so do Miss Americana and the Heartbreak Prince.

It's all about dealing with an unfriendly world – but doing it with your head up, chest out and a smile on your face.

HOLDING ONTO HOPE

Finally, let's talk about the "Go! Fight! Win!" cheerleader-esque chant we hear during the bridge of the song.

This is hopecore in action – a pinnacle moment of feminist writing. Hope is at the heart of feminist literature because it envisions a future where change is possible. This song turns into a rallying cry, reminding us that the fight isn't over, and victory is on the horizon.

Next time you listen to "Miss Americana & The Heartbreak Prince", know that you're blasting a song that's loaded with pure female empowerment. It's catchy, sure, but it's also a mighty statement!

✶ Have you seen Taylor Swift's documentary "Miss Americana"? How do you think the film ties into the way she challenges gender roles in "Miss Americana & The Heartbreak Prince"?

RECLAIMING "SLUT"

The song ""Slut!"" gives us a different take on Taylor Swift's approach to feminism.

Taylor revealed in a voice memo on Tumblr that it came down to including either ""Slut!"" or "Blank Space" on the original *1989* album. While both songs take a swipe at the media's portrayal of her – and women in general – ""Slut!"" likely stayed in the vault for a decade because its title and themes were considered less-than-modest at the time, even if that's no longer the case for Taylor now.

Yet, in this song, Taylor masterfully reclaims a word that is used to shame women and turns it into a defiant message. It's a great example of how she challenges societal norms and embraces the complexities of female identity in her music.

FEMINIST LYRICS

For each of the feminist themes below, write a set of lyrics from the song ""Slut!"" that you think captures that theme.

* **Reclaiming language:**

* **Challenging social expectations:**

* **Expressing female desire:**

* **Navigating a patriarchal society:**

* **Empowerment and agency:**

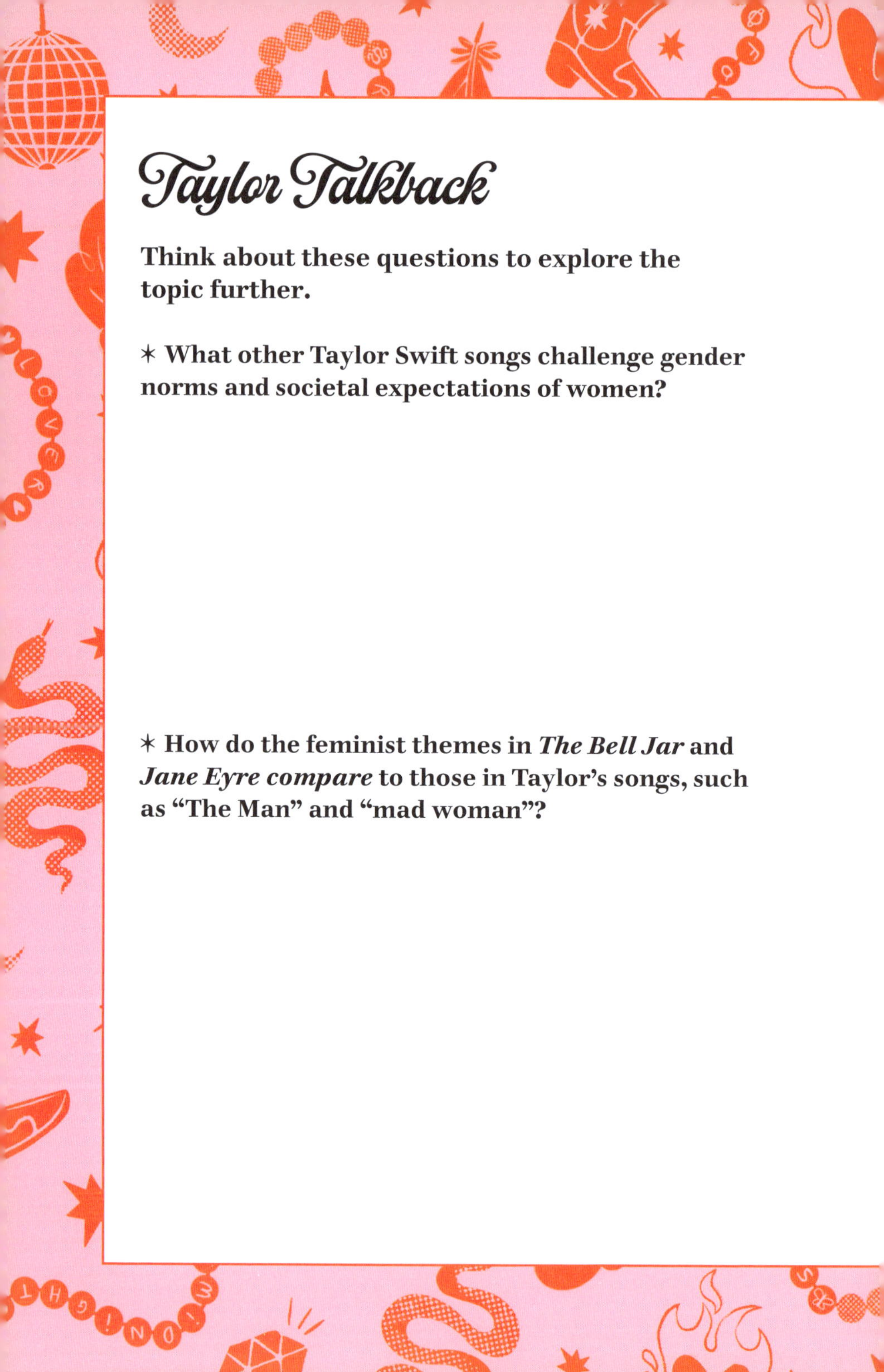

Taylor Talkback

Think about these questions to explore the topic further.

✶ What other Taylor Swift songs challenge gender norms and societal expectations of women?

✶ How do the feminist themes in *The Bell Jar* and *Jane Eyre compare* to those in Taylor's songs, such as "The Man" and "mad woman"?

✶ How do these older novels still connect with today's discussions about gender and equality?

✶ How have the feminist themes explored in this chapter played a part in your own life?

CHAPTER 5
Rebel With a Cause

Themes of rebellion and social commentary in Taylor Swift's music

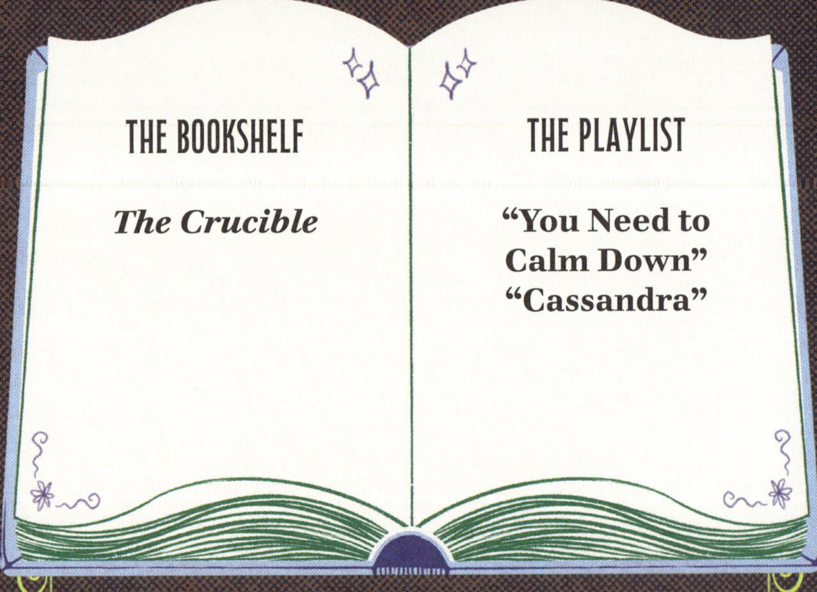

Queue up this chapter's songs to listen and follow along!

Social Commentary & Rebellion

Rebellion and social commentary are often explored in literature through characters who challenge authority and tradition.

Authors use their fictional works to discuss and critique injustice and inequality. They encourage readers to think about the problems in the world around them and figure out how to fix them.

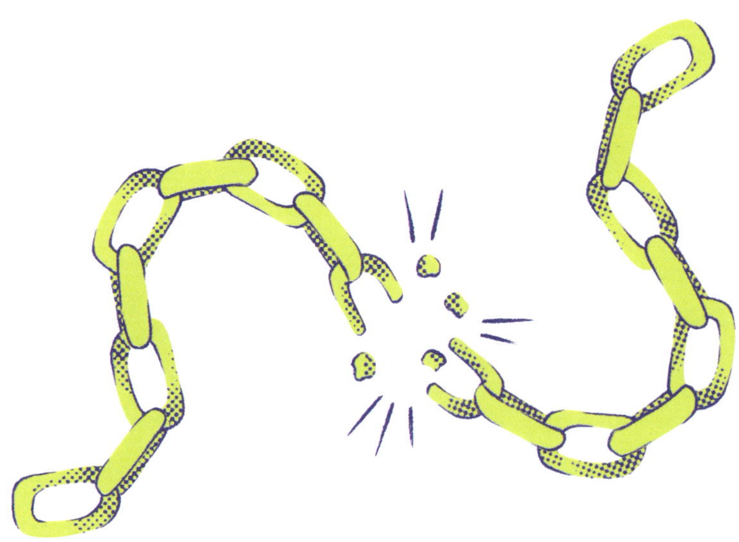

REBELLION 101

When it comes to novels about social commentary or rebellion, you're likely to spot these key elements:

* **Allegories:** stories written as metaphors to tackle big social and political issues.
* **Dystopian settings:** grim imagined futures that show what might happen if our problems spin out of control.
* **Outsider protagonists:** people who stand out from the crowd, either because they think differently or they're ready to break the rules.
* **Conflict in power dynamics:** either between an individual and society, or between those who are powerful and those who dare to resist.
* **Satire:** a healthy dose of humorous exaggeration that points out society's flaws.
* **Symbolism:** represents big ideas, like freedom or oppression.
* **Moral questions:** to make us think about what's right, what's wrong and the state of our own society.
* **Foreshadowing:** dropping hints about what's to come (like a literary Easter egg).

Let's be honest – there's a reason why these kinds of books are often our favourites. They serve up just the right amount of nail-biting tension and "stick it to the man" energy. Case in point: *The Hunger Games*. It's hard to resist a story where the underdogs take on the powers that be ... and maybe even win.

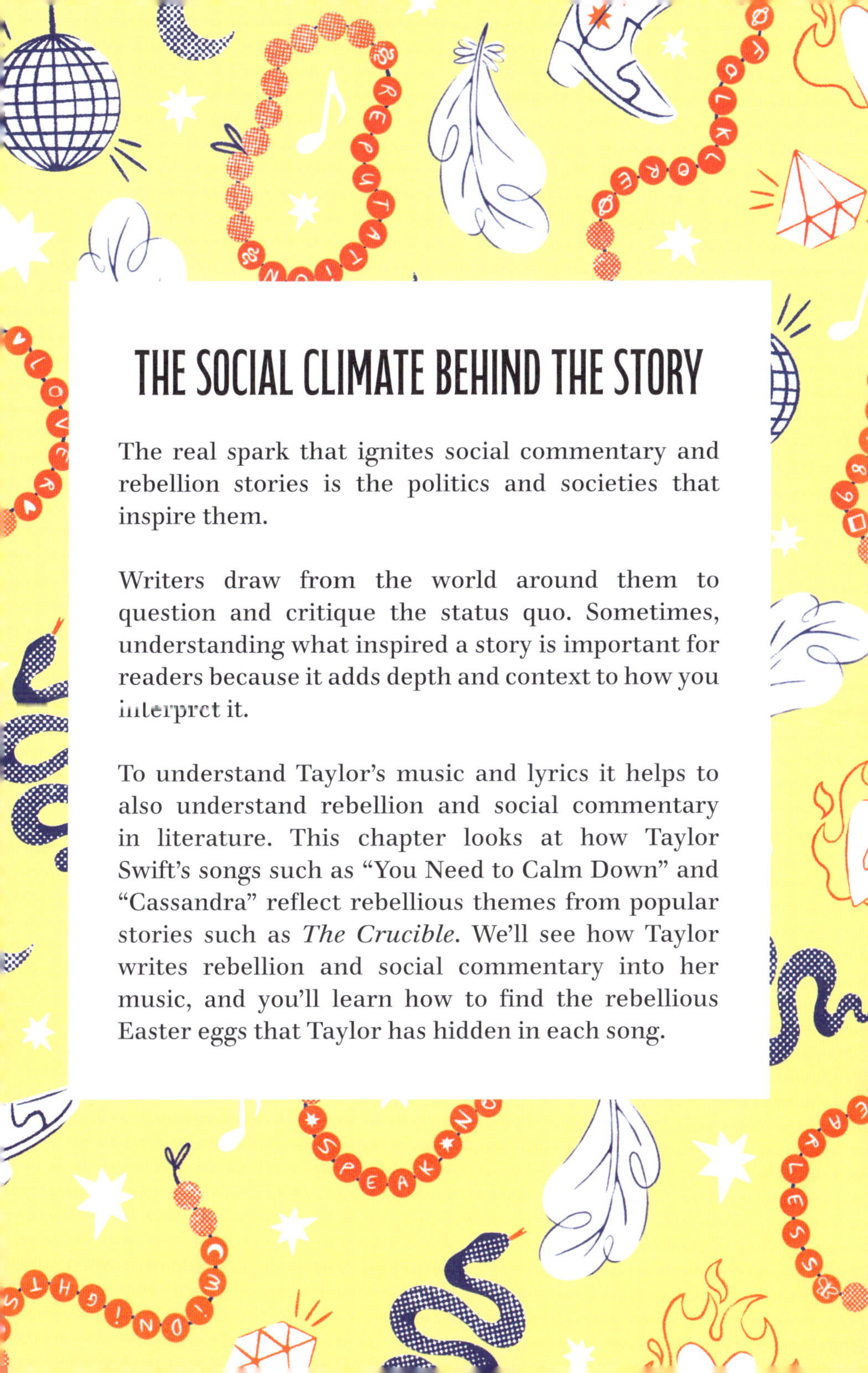

THE SOCIAL CLIMATE BEHIND THE STORY

The real spark that ignites social commentary and rebellion stories is the politics and societies that inspire them.

Writers draw from the world around them to question and critique the status quo. Sometimes, understanding what inspired a story is important for readers because it adds depth and context to how you interpret it.

To understand Taylor's music and lyrics it helps to also understand rebellion and social commentary in literature. This chapter looks at how Taylor Swift's songs such as "You Need to Calm Down" and "Cassandra" reflect rebellious themes from popular stories such as *The Crucible*. We'll see how Taylor writes rebellion and social commentary into her music, and you'll learn how to find the rebellious Easter eggs that Taylor has hidden in each song.

Swift Prep

Let's begin with a few questions to focus your mind.

✶ Which form of art is the stronger tool for critiquing society: music or literature? Why?

* **If you were to write a song or book today that comments on society, which current event or issue would inspire it?**

* **When you think of Taylor Swift, do you see her as a rebel, a social commentator or something else entirely?**

The Crucible
By Arthur Miller

SWIFTSNOTES

Maybe you have seen the play or you read it in class. Either way, here is a run-down of *The Crucible* by Arthur Miller, written in the 1950s:

✶ In Salem, Massachusetts, 1692, Abigail Williams and her circle claim they are being possessed by witches and start accusing anyone who gets in their way of witchcraft.

✶ John Proctor, a respected farmer, gets pulled into the chaos when his wife, Elizabeth, is accused of witchcraft.

✶ Accusations fly everywhere, and the trials spiral out of control. Salem's justice system is a mess because it relies on weak evidence and forced confessions. The town is consumed by fear.

✶ At first, Reverend Hale believes in the presence of witches, but over time, he starts noticing that things don't add up. Eventually, he urges the accused witches to go along with it and confess, even though they're lying, just to save their lives.

✶ John Proctor has a tough moral decision to make: confess to witchcraft and live, or stand by his principles and face execution. He ultimately refuses to admit to witchcraft and ends up being hanged.

✶ Salem is in shambles, haunted by the fallout of its own madness and the deaths of innocent people, but John Proctor's act of courage helps expose the truth and inspires others to stand up against lies.

WHAT INSPIRED THE CRUCIBLE?

This play is a cautionary tale about how panic, power trips and blatant lies can cause chaos and destruction in society.

It isn't really about witches. Arthur Miller wrote *The Crucible* during the 1950s, using the Salem witch trials as a metaphor for McCarthyism – a time when the US government, led by Senator Joseph McCarthy, accused people of being communists without real proof. Just like in the play, fear and false accusations spiralled out of control, ruined lives and divided communities.

THE CRUCIBLE
&
You Need to Calm Down

Just like understanding the context of *The Crucible* helps us understand its message, it's important to know what was going on when Taylor Swift released her anthem "You Need to Calm Down" in support of the LGBTQ+ community.

In early 2019, back in Taylor's home state of Tennessee, the government rolled out a bunch of laws targeting LGBTQ+ people. These included attempts to block same-sex couples from adopting children and to restrict transgender people's access to bathrooms.

These laws sparked outrage, as they attacked the rights of LGBTQ+ people.

It's likely that Taylor channelled her frustration with these laws into her writing. "You Need to Calm Down" stands up for LGBTQ+ individuals and calls out those who unfairly judge them. By cleverly mentioning organizations such as GLAAD – which promotes acceptance and understanding of LGBTQ+ people – Taylor reinforces her support for the community.

It's a modern-day parallel to *The Crucible*, and the way it exposed the dangers of fear and unfair accusations during the era of anti-Communist hysteria.

The Crucible and "You Need to Calm Down" both explore themes of judgement.Take Judge Danforth's line from Act III of *The Crucible*: "I have seen your power; you will not deny it! You have seen the Devil, you have made compact with Lucifer, have you not?" In modern English, this means, "I know what you're up to! You've made a deal with the Devil, haven't you?"

Danforth uses this accusation to pressure a young local woman, Mary Warren, into confessing to witchcraft, even though there is no evidence against her. It's a prime example of rushing to judgement without proof, driven purely by fear.

Now, think about the lyrics from verses one and two of "You Need to Calm Down". Someone Taylor doesn't know is insulting her and her LGBTQ+ friends online.

It draws a parallel with Judge Danforth's accusation. Both outbursts involve making assumptions without any real understanding of the person or situation they are attacking. Whether it's a fictional witch hunt or a modern-day troll, both the play and the song remind us that judging a book by its cover hurts everyone involved.

✶ If "You Need To Calm Down" was written about witch hunts instead of LGBTQ+ rights, how might the lyrics change? Rewrite a few lines of the song to reflect themes from *The Crucible*.

✦ How do you respond to things you're scared of or don't understand? Do you seek out information, talk to someone you trust, write in a journal or do something else to process your feelings?

YOU REALLY DO NEED TO CALM DOWN

By the way ... throwing shade doesn't make the "gay" go away. "You Need To Calm Down" is a Taylor-fied reminder to leave the judgement behind.

John Proctor shares his own iconic version of this reminder in *The Crucible*: "I speak my own sins; I cannot judge another. I have no tongue for it."

Taylor and Proctor show us that everyone has their own lanes to stay in and their own challenges to face, so pointing fingers and judging others is just not the way to go. Standing up for yourself and staying true to who you are is what really matters!

✶ Which scenes from the "You Need to Calm Down" music video parallel the hysteria and judgement in *The Crucible*?

THE CRUCIBLE & *Cassandra*

Who's Cassandra, anyway? To fully understand this song, let's start with a quick lesson in Greek mythology.

Cassandra was the daughter of King Priam and Queen Hecuba of Troy and was given the gift of seeing the future by the god Apollo. However, when she rejected Apollo's romantic advances, he cursed her so that no one would believe her predictions.

Despite forecasting the fall of Troy and other disasters, Cassandra was dismissed. Troy was destroyed when the Trojans ignored her warnings about the Greek wooden horse, and Cassandra was taken as a prisoner of war, ultimately meeting a brutal death.

✶ How does "Cassandra" add new layers to the Greek myth? Which lyrics stand out to you and why?

STICKS AND STONES

In a slightly more subdued way, Taylor's song "Cassandra" explores the same themes of fear and judgement that we see in "You Need to Calm Down".

The repeated pre-chorus of the song paints a scene straight out of *The Crucible*, with riots in the streets, people screaming for witches and throwing stones.

The lyrics echo the same kind of chaos Abigail Williams creates in Salem when she walks around screaming that Sarah Good, Goody Osborn and Bridget Bishop were all practicing witchcraft.

✶ What other Taylor Swift songs explore themes of witch-like persecution or being treated like a villain?

THE PRICE YOU PAY

Let's pour one out for Cassandra and another for John Proctor, because one more thing they have in common is that they face serious consequences for sticking to their truths.

In *The Crucible*, Proctor refuses to give in to the witch hysteria and chooses to keep his integrity over admitting to a false confession – even though it costs him his life. Similarly, in Taylor's "Cassandra", just like in the Greek myth, she tries to warn everyone about what's coming but is silenced for speaking up.

Each of these characters show their guts as they stand up for what they believe in, no matter what it costs.

Taylor Talkback

Think about these questions to explore the topic further.

✶ What other Taylor Swift songs challenge tradition or advocate for something meaningful?

✶ What do you think the context was that caused her to write those songs?

✶ **Symbols are a big part of social commentary in literature. Are there any symbols or symbolic words in Taylor Swift's songs that might represent a form of rebellion, or social commentary?**

✶ **Do you think musicians such as Taylor Swift and writers such as Arthur Miller have an obligation to use their work to comment on society?**

CHAPTER 6

Once Upon a Taylor ...

The influence of fairy tales in Taylor Swift's music

Queue up this chapter's songs to listen and follow along!

Folklore and Fairy Tales

A fairy tale is a short story belonging to the folklore genre, which usually features magic and mystical beings.

These stories are rich in moral lessons, teaching us the difference between good and evil. These tales from far-off magical lands can act as metaphors, helping the reader interpret what's good and evil in the present day.

They inspire us to rise above the challenges and fears that life throws our way. They soothe us when we're overwhelmed. They help us understand that in our own lives there are woods and there are wolves, but if we are clever (and kind), we will survive.

The Tale of the Shipwrecked Sailor

Have you ever heard of the oldest known fairy tale, *The Tale of the Shipwrecked Sailor*? It's from ancient Egypt, c. 2000 BCE.

A sailor finds himself stranded on a mysterious island after a strong storm destroys his ship. On the island, he meets a giant serpent who has been alone for years, waiting for its lost family.

The sailor and the serpent share their fears and dreams. They bond over their longing for friendship and the hope of going home. As their friendship grows, the serpent reveals a boat is hidden on the island and promises the sailor a safe trip back to his loved ones.

The sailor departs, leaving the serpent behind, forever grateful for their time together. The serpent watches him leave, feeling a little sad but also at peace, knowing it has made a friend. The sailor returns home and shares the story of the island and the kind serpent. Meanwhile, the serpent stays on the island, hopeful that more new friends will come.

This fairy tale uses the serpent as a fantastical example of exploring the comfort of knowing we don't have to face difficult things alone. Like many fairy tales, it shows that hope can be found in unexpected places and helps us deal with real-life challenges.

The Tale of the Shipwrecked ~~Sailor~~ Taylor

Sound familiar?

Taylor's *folklore* and *evermore* albums, which were written during the tough times of the COVID-19 pandemic, feel like modern fairy tales.

The titular track of the "evermore" album is all about clinging to hope, and it uses shipwreck imagery to symbolize tough times, just like in *The Tale of The Shipwrecked Sailor*.

To understand Taylor's music and lyrics, it helps to understand fairy tales. This chapter looks at how Taylor Swift's songs, such as "gold rush", "Bejeweled" and "Wonderland", reflect common themes from popular fairy tales such as "The Fisherman and His Wife" and other Grimms' fairy tales and the story *Alice's Adventures in Wonderland*. We'll see how Taylor uses these fairy tales in her music, and you'll learn how to find the folkloric Easter eggs she has hidden in each song.

Let's begin with a few questions to focus your mind.

* What fairy tales captivated you as a child? Which elements or themes in those stories still feel relevant in your life today?

* Which Taylor Swift songs feel like fairy tales to you? What magical elements make them so enchanting?

* **Pick a Taylor Swift song that parallels a fairy tale you know. How does she reimagine the story to add depth to her music?**

* **Does this connection make you see the original story in a different light? If so, how?**

The Fisherman & His Wife

By the Brothers Grimm

SWIFTSNOTES

If you aren't familiar with the Grimm brothers' classic story "The Fisherman and His Wife", no worries! Here's a crash course:

✶ A poor fisherman catches a talking flounder who claims he's actually a prince under a spell. Feeling sorry for him, the fisherman lets him go.

✶ When the fisherman tells his wife about the flounder, she says, "Go back and ask him for a nice little cottage instead of our rundown shack."

✶ At first, the wife is happy with the new cottage, but eventually, she gets bored. She sends her husband back multiple times to ask for something fancier each time. They move from a cottage to a full-blown castle.

✶ It doesn't stop there. She wants to be the boss of everything – first a king, (she specifically asks to be king), then an emperor and even a pope, and the magical talking flounder makes it all happen.

✶ Finally, she wants to rule the heavens, asking to become like God. The fisherman is really hesitant but asks the flounder anyway.

✶ The flounder, annoyed with the wife's behavior, zaps them back to their old, shabby hut, stripping them of everything they had gained.

THE FISHERMAN & HIS WIFE
&
gold rush

The song "gold rush" is an *evermore*-era gem that evokes a sense of enchantment, desire and transition from ordinary to extraordinary. Much like the Grimm brothers' fairy tale of "The Fisherman and His Wife", the song is heavy on themes of:

- **The desire for more**
- **The consequences of greed**
- **Transformation**

DESIRE FOR MORE

Listen closely to "gold rush". Taylor talks all about wanting beauty and wealth that she can't have – because it's all tied to a fantasy she knows isn't real. Similarly, "The Fisherman and His Wife" is about the wife's insatiable desire, as she keeps asking the magical fish for more and more, getting lost in the dream of having it all.

CONSEQUENCES OF GREED

Both "gold rush" and "The Fisherman and His Wife" show what can happen when your desires get out of control. In the song, Taylor talks about how exciting desire can feel – like flying – until it suddenly turns and leaves you crushed by the weight of it. It tricks you! And it is similar to how the wife's growing greed in the Grimm brothers' fairy tale causes the couple to lose everything. The song and the story warn about the risks of unchecked desire and the bad things that can happen.

*** Which lyric or lyrics from "gold rush" best capture the thrill and fallout of unchecked desire?**

✶ **What do these lyrics make you think or feel about the theme of greed?**

TRANSFORMATION

In "gold rush", Taylor imagines a dreamlike transformation of changing someone's life into a story or folklore. Similarly, in "The Fisherman and His Wife", the wife wishes to change her life and status to something totally different. But just like the wife's new life falls apart, in "gold rush" Taylor shifts from imagining a magical life to stepping back and seeing it for what it really is – a fantasy. Ironically, Taylor and the fisherman's wife both end up back where they started, living their ordinary, unmagical lives. The stories show how desire can transform illusion into reality, but reality always takes over in the end.

✶ How does Taylor's change in perspective in "gold rush" – from fantasy to reality – affect how you see the song's message about desire?

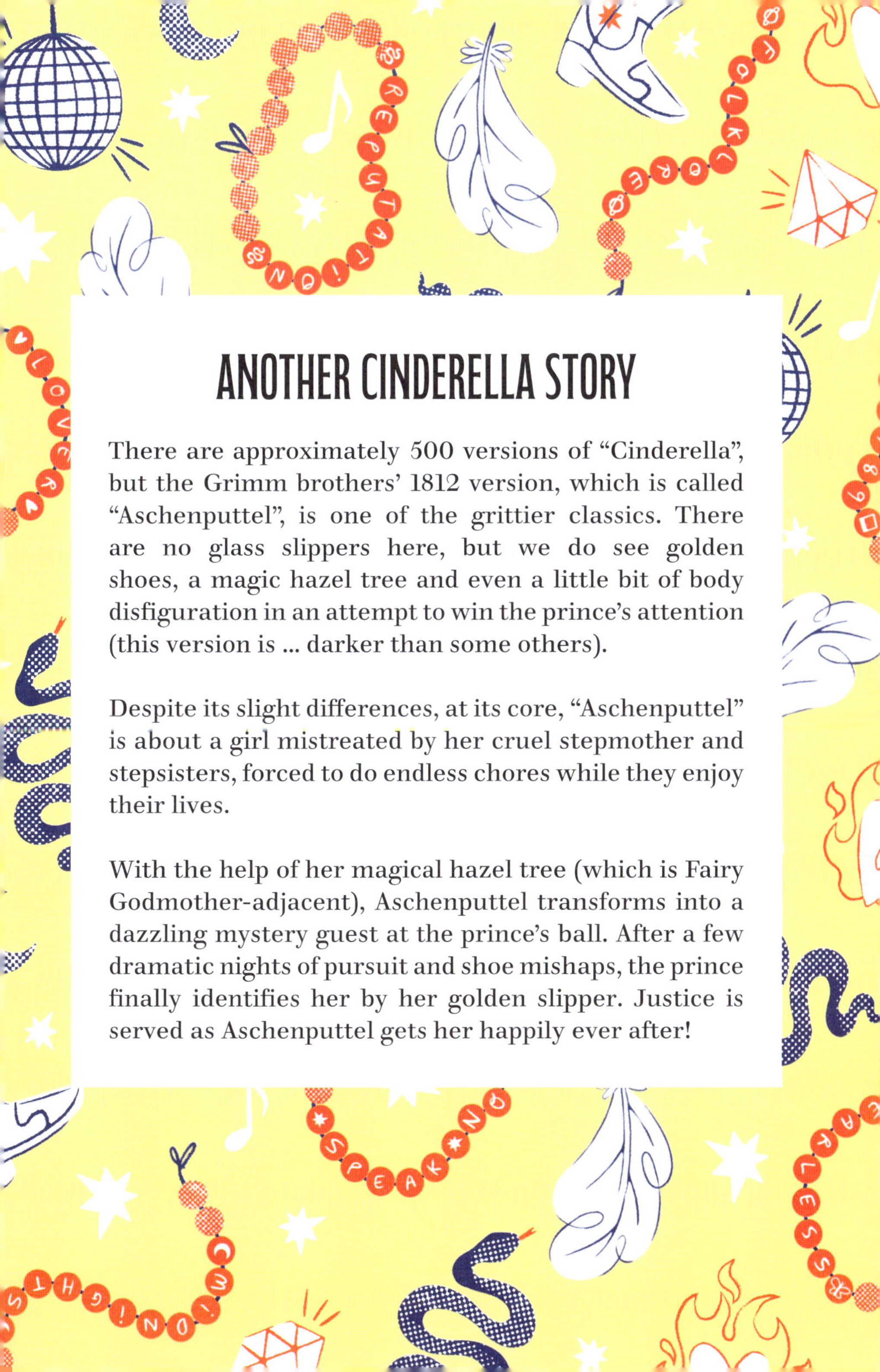

ANOTHER CINDERELLA STORY

There are approximately 500 versions of "Cinderella", but the Grimm brothers' 1812 version, which is called "Aschenputtel", is one of the grittier classics. There are no glass slippers here, but we do see golden shoes, a magic hazel tree and even a little bit of body disfiguration in an attempt to win the prince's attention (this version is ... darker than some others).

Despite its slight differences, at its core, "Aschenputtel" is about a girl mistreated by her cruel stepmother and stepsisters, forced to do endless chores while they enjoy their lives.

With the help of her magical hazel tree (which is Fairy Godmother-adjacent), Aschenputtel transforms into a dazzling mystery guest at the prince's ball. After a few dramatic nights of pursuit and shoe mishaps, the prince finally identifies her by her golden slipper. Justice is served as Aschenputtel gets her happily ever after!

CINDERELLA & *Bejeweled*

Did you catch the "Cinderella" reference in Taylor's "Bejeweled" music video? It borrows from the classic rags-to-riches tale but with a lighter twist compared to the Grimm brothers' version.

This chapter's Music Video Muse hits all the key points of another Grimm brothers' classic:

- **Dismissive family (complete with an evil step-mother)**
- **Magical transformation – in this case, into a sparkly outfit**
- **Fabulous fairy godmother**
- **Grand party or ball**
- **Happy ending – in this case, with Taylor winning everything ... the prince, the castle and the whole kingdom**

In Taylor's version of "Cinderella", her happy ending involves ditching the prince and having independence over her own life, rather than relying on a man to love her. In comparison, the climax of "Aschenputtel" – and most other "Cinderella" stories – revolves around the prince rescuing Cindy from her awful life.

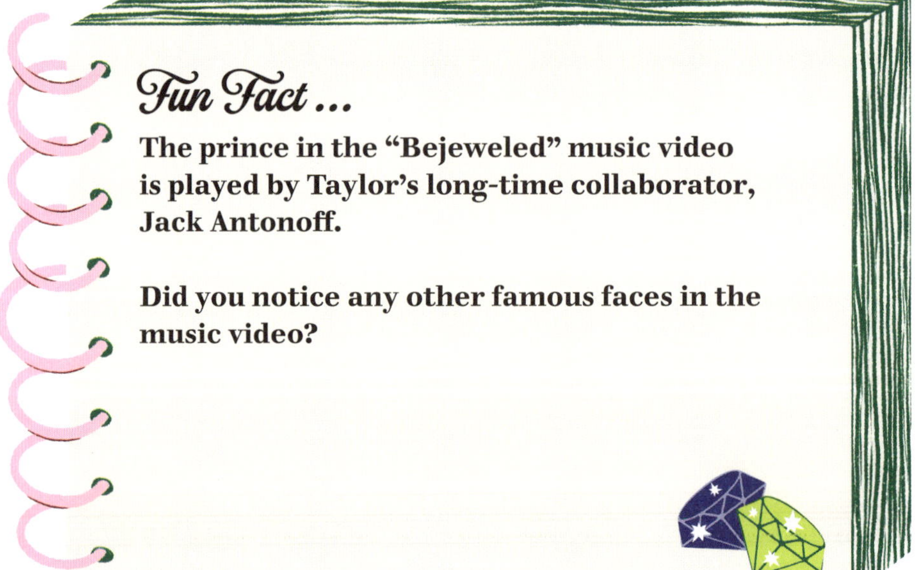

Fun Fact ...

The prince in the "Bejeweled" music video is played by Taylor's long-time collaborator, Jack Antonoff.

Did you notice any other famous faces in the music video?

✶ **What does Taylor's version of "Cinderella" say about the various roles and goals traditionally assigned to characters in fairy tales (particularly female characters)?**

✶ **How does Taylor's version of "Cinderella" in "Bejeweled" bring the classic fairy tale into the 21st century?**

Alice's Adventures
in Wonderland
By Lewis Carroll

SWIFTSNOTES

Haven't read Lewis Carroll's 1865 story *Alice's Adventures in Wonderland*, or watched the Disney version? No problem! Here is a quick crash course:

* Alice, a curious young girl, spots a rabbit wearing a coat and pocket watch. She follows him down a rabbit hole into a bizarre place called Wonderland.

* Wonderland is wild. Alice meets a bunch of weird characters, including a sleepy dormouse who tells odd stories, the vanishing Cheshire Cat and a caterpillar who's *very* into hookah.

* Alice crashes a tea party hosted by the Mad Hatter and the March Hare. It's nonsensical and chaotic and the tea never actually gets poured.

* As she wanders through Wonderland, Alice struggles to control her size. She keeps eating and drinking things that make her either huge or tiny.

* Alice ends up facing the Queen of Hearts in a croquet match. The queen loves yelling, "Off with their heads!" The game is played with flamingos as mallets, and the balls are hedgehogs, naturally.

* Alice ends up at a trial where the Knave of Hearts is accused of stealing tarts. The trial makes zero sense. Just as things get heated, Alice grows super tall and finds herself waking up on the riverbank, realising it might have all been a dream.

ALICE'S ADVENTURES IN WONDERLAND
&
Wonderland

There are no surprises here: Taylor Swift's song "Wonderland" directly references Lewis Carroll's *Alice's Adventures in Wonderland.*

✶ Can you list all the lyrics in "Wonderland" that echo the original story?

Beyond lyrics, this *1989* bonus track stands out for its playfulness and whimsicality. The song includes several themes from the original story by Lewis Carroll, such as the tension between fantasy and reality, the complexity of love, the allure of escapism and a sense of nostalgia that contrasts with the modern, pop-focused vibe of the rest of the album.

FANTASY VS. REALITY

The song "Wonderland", like *Alice's Adventures in Wonderland*, is more focused on a dreamy, fantasy world than real life. Its whimsical and surreal tone contrasts with other songs from the *1989* era, such as "Blank Space" and "Style", which are more grounded in reality. Other songs from the album explore real-life love stories and how the media saw Taylor Swift at the time the album was released.

✶ Do the lyrics of "Wonderland" remind you of any of your own real-life experiences?

COMPLEXITY VS. CLARITY

The use of imagery from *Alice's Adventures in Wonderland* in "Wonderland" adds layers of complexity and ambiguity to the song. It invites you to interpret the metaphors. This mirrors the chaotic and unpredictable nature of Wonderland, where nothing is as it seems. In contrast, other songs from the *1989* album, such as "Shake It Off" or "Bad Blood", focus on more clear-cut themes, such as self-confidence and personal feuds, making their messages easier to grasp compared to the more abstract storytelling in "Wonderland".

⁎ What metaphors are written in the lyrics of "Wonderland"? List them here and explain what they might mean.

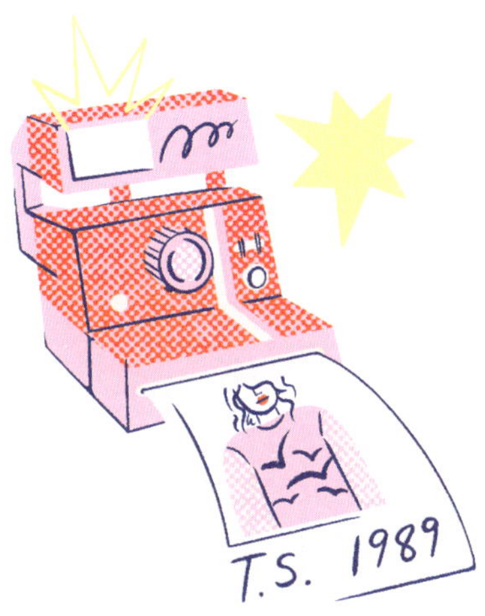

ESCAPISM VS. CONFRONTATION

"Wonderland", much like the book, offers a place to escape to. It transports you to a fantastical world where you can ponder the nature of love and reality, and it explores the feeling of being so caught up in something magical that you lose sight of what's real. However, other songs from the era, such as "Out of the Woods", confront real-life challenges and anxieties, such as addressing the difficulties of a toxic relationship head on.

✶ Why do you think Taylor included "Wonderland" on her *1989* album?

NOSTALGIA VS. MODERNITY

Overall, the imagery in "Wonderland" creates a nostalgia and timelessness that reminds us of a classic tale, which is very different from the heavy 2014, pop sound, Tumblr-girl experiences and New York attitude of the rest of *1989*.

✶ Are there any other songs or lyrics in Taylor's discography that reference *Alice's Adventures in Wonderland*?

Taylor Talkback

Think about these questions to explore the topic further.

✶ How do you connect with fantasy-esque songs such as "Wonderland" and "gold rush"? What do they mean to you?

✶ Taylor's albums *folklore* and *evermore* have a notably different storytelling style from her other music. What other characteristics of fairy tales do you see in these two albums that we haven't covered in this chapter?

✶ If you could see a fairy tale turned into a Taylor Swift song, which one would you choose? Can you think of what some of the lyrics for that song could be?

CHAPTER 7
Mirrors & Masks

Exploring themes of identity and self-perception in Taylor Swift's music

THE BOOKSHELF

The Picture of Dorian Gray
The Importance of Being Earnest

THE PLAYLIST

"mirrorball"
"Anti-Hero"
"Clara Bow"

Queue up this chapter's songs to listen and follow along!

Confronting Identity

Art is like a mirror – it shows us who we are.

But sometimes, it distorts the truth, and this forces us to confront uncomfortable realities about ourselves.

In books and other literature, it's common to read about characters who struggle with their identities, torn between how they perceive themselves and how the rest of the world views them.

This struggle usually pushes us to take a closer look at ourselves and the roles we play in society.

THE NAME'S WILDE, OSCAR WILDE

Oscar Wilde set the gold standard for using art to explore identity and self-perception. He was far from your typical 19th-century writer!

Wilde was a master of wit, with a flair for flamboyance, and a serious talent for exposing society's moral blind spots. Through his clever plays and haunting stories, Wilde had a knack for peeling back the masks people wear and the ones society creates to reveal the raw and uncomfortable truths beneath them.

THE NAME'S SWIFT, TAYLOR SWIFT

Like Wilde, Taylor Swift has a gift for taking off the masks we wear. She does this by singing about her own struggles, which makes her music relatable.

A good example is her devastating track five from *Lover* (as though all of her track fives aren't devastating). In "The Archer", Taylor talks about the tension between how others see her and what she's feeling inside. It's like pulling back the string of a bow – the more you pull, the more the pressure builds until it has to be released.

The music here mirrors a panic attack, with a slow build of synths that becomes more intense as the song goes on. By the time she hits the repetitive, almost frantic bridge, the lyrics reflect her fear of being truly seen.

Taylor uses her music to show us how complicated the relationship is between who we are and how others see us. "The Archer" is about the fear of being seen for who you really are, and her music pushes us to face that fear and search for the truth deep inside.

To understand Taylor's music and lyrics, it helps to understand themes of identity and self-perception in literature. This chapter looks at how Taylor Swift's songs such as "mirrorball", "Anti-Hero" and "Clara Bow" reflect common themes from Oscar Wilde's works such as *The Picture of Dorian Gray* and *The Importance of Being Earnest*. We'll see how Taylor uses these themes in her music, and you'll learn how to find the Easter eggs Taylor has hidden in each song.

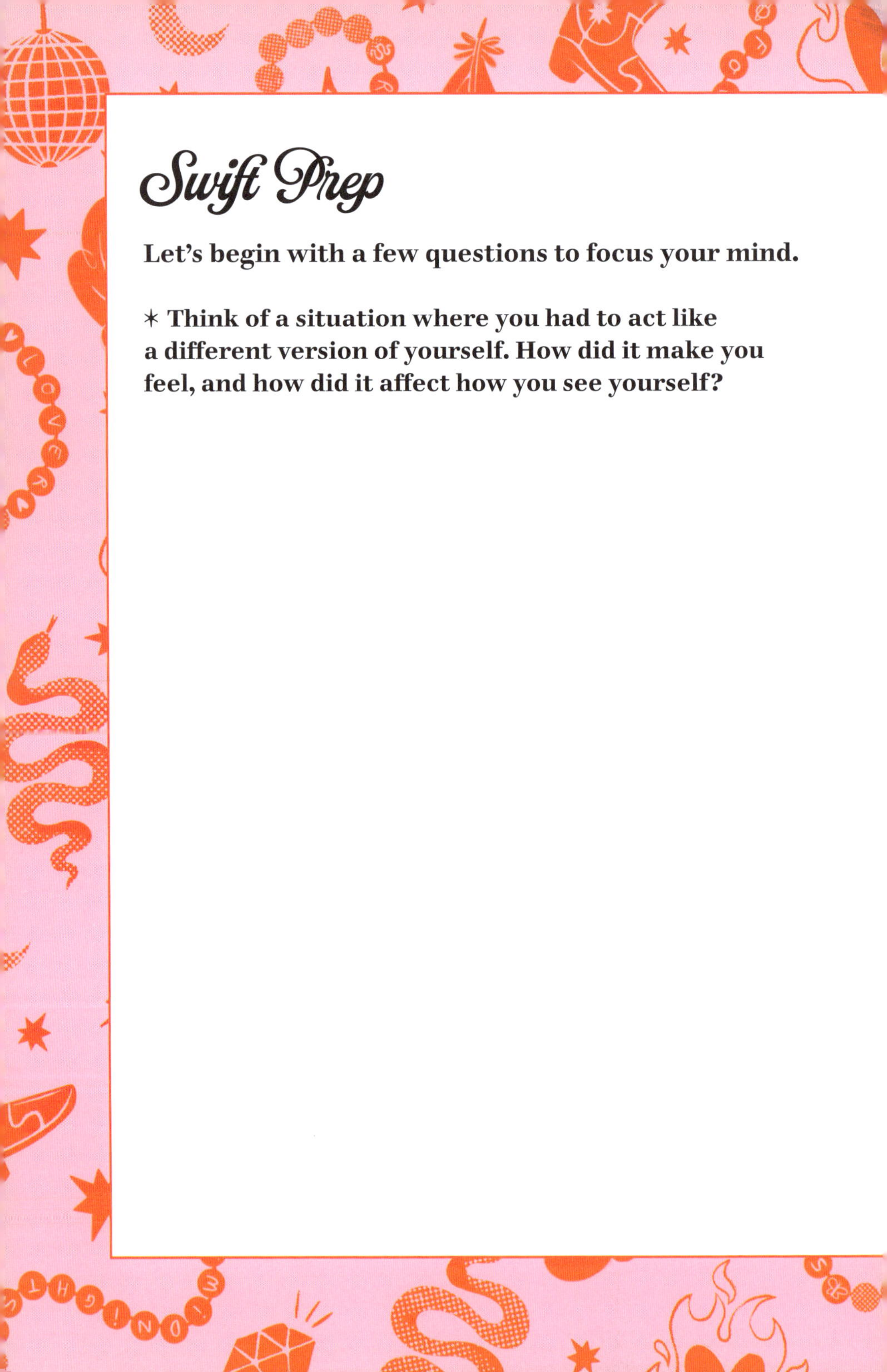

Swift Prep

Let's begin with a few questions to focus your mind.

✶ Think of a situation where you had to act like a different version of yourself. How did it make you feel, and how did it affect how you see yourself?

* **Which persona, or "era", of Taylor's is your favourite, and why? What makes you connect with that version of her?**

* **Are there any Taylor Swift songs that made you see yourself differently the first time you heard them? How did they change the way you view yourself?**

The Picture of Dorian Gray
By Oscar Wilde

SWIFTSNOTES

If you aren't familiar with Wilde's only published novel from 1890, that's alright! Here is a quick rundown on *The Picture of Dorian Gray*:

* Basil Hallward paints a portrait of Dorian Gray, a charming young man.

* Dorian meets Lord Henry Wotton, who convinces him to live a life of pleasure. Dorian wishes his portrait would age instead of him so he can keep living this way forever.

* Dorian starts living a reckless and indulgent life, and the portrait starts revealing the ugly truth of his actions. Because of this, Dorian stays young and handsome.

* His reckless behaviour ends up hurting people around him, including Sibyl Vane, an actress who takes her own life after Dorian rejects her.

* Dorian feels guilty and horrified by his picture, so he tries to turn his life around, but too much damage has already been done.

* Dorian tries to destroy the portrait in a desperate attempt to escape his guilt. This backfires and leads to his own death, as his body finally ages and takes on all of the ugliness he had been hiding.

THE PICTURE OF DORIAN GRAY
&
mirrorball

The song "mirrorball" is about the pressure to fit in and show a perfect image of yourself to the world. The mirror ball metaphor represents someone constantly changing and adapting to meet the expectations of others.

In *The Picture of Dorian Gray*, Dorian's portrait becomes a mirror to his soul. It shows off all the moral decay that's happening to him, caused by his hedonistic and selfish lifestyle. While Dorian indulges in pleasure and ignores the consequences of his actions, his portrait gets uglier and reflects the truth he's hiding from the world.

Just like Dorian hides his real self behind a pretty face, Taylor in "mirrorball" sings about the pressure to keep spinning, shining and maintaining an image that dazzles the world, even if it means losing pieces of her true self along the way.

✶ **Which lyrics in "mirrorball" show the pressure that the narrator feels to keep performing?**

DORIAN GRAY VS. TAYLOR SWIFT

Dorian and Taylor struggle with more than just their image. They also grapple with:

- **Desire for approval**
- **The cost of perfection**
- **Vulnerability and exposure**

DESIRE FOR APPROVAL

The need to be liked pushes Dorian, and Taylor in "mirrorball", to extreme lengths. Dorian has to rely on a picture of himself to maintain his looks because of his obsession with being young and beautiful. Taylor talks about constantly changing to make everyone else happy and promises to reflect everything back at them that they want to see. Both characters struggle to be everything for everyone, and this causes them to lose touch with who they really are.

✶ What parallels can you draw between the metaphor of the mirror ball in the song and the portrait in the book?

COST OF PERFECTION

Perfection comes at a steep price for Dorian and Taylor. Dorian sacrifices his morals to stay beautiful, but his reckless behaviour ultimately leads to his death. Taylor, on the other hand, is exhausted from keeping up with society's standards.

Pay attention to what she's telling us in the bridge of "mirrorball" – she's admitting that maintaining the "Taylor Swift" image isn't easy for her, and it sometimes takes a lot of energy for her to put on this performance. In both cases, the need for perfection causes Dorian and Taylor to lose themselves and become trapped in the images they worked so hard to create.

✶ Which other Taylor Swift songs explore the idea that being famous can be exhausting?

VULNERABILITY AND EXPOSURE

Both Taylor in "mirrorball" and Dorian wrestle with the fear of being truly seen. Dorian hides his ugliness behind a mask of beauty, while Taylor walks along a delicate tightrope of public approval – she has to be perfect!

Her difficulty with this balancing act is made clear when she admits she's still on a tightrope, desperately trying to keep everyone entertained. It sounds exhausting striving to be something you're not, and "mirrorball" captures that feeling beautifully.

✶ Do you relate to the pressure Taylor describes in "mirrorball" to keep everyone happy and entertained? Which lyrics stand out to you the most?

The Importance of Being Earnest
By Oscar Wilde
ERNEST
ERNEST

SWIFTSNOTES

Maybe you've read his other work, but you're not familiar with Oscar Wilde's 1895 farce, *The Importance of Being Earnest.* No worries! Here is an overview:

✶ Algernon Moncrieff is a charming bachelor, and Jack Worthing is a respectable gentleman with a country estate. Both lead secret double lives – Jack pretends to have a brother named Ernest as an excuse to visit the city, and Algernon invents a sick friend named Bunbury to escape social obligations.

✶ As a joke, both Algernon and Jack pretend to go by the name "Ernest" to avoid their responsibilities and find love.

✶ Jack plans to marry Gwendolen Fairfax, who loves the name Ernest. Meanwhile, Algernon, also pretending to be called Ernest, courts Jack's ward, Cecily. The two women meet and gush over their fiancés, amazed by the uncanny coincidence that both men share the same name.

✶ Jack and Gwendolyn's marriage is jeopardized when Lady Bracknell, Gwendolyn's mother, discovers that Jack was adopted after being found in a handbag at a train station as a baby. She demands he find his real family.

✶ The truth about the men's double lives comes out when Gwendolyn and Cecily discover Algernon and Jack's secret through a series of comedic mix-ups.

✶ Through her investigation, Lady Bracknell reveals Jack's birth family, and that Jack is actually Algernon's long-lost older brother and that his real name is Ernest! This clears up all the confusion about their identities, and Jack and Gwendolen and Algernon and Cecily all get happily engaged.

BUNBURYING

The term "bunburying" is when someone creates a fictional person to escape their social duties and live a double life. Oscar Wilde introduced this idea in *The Importance of Being Earnest*: Algernon invents an imaginary sick friend named Mr Bunbury who he occasionally has to take care of. This fictional friend gives Algernon the perfect excuse to skip out on boring, elite social events and instead enjoy time on his own.

Jack and Algernon use their Ernest personas in a similar way. Being "Ernest" allows them to live double lives and do whatever they want, free from their usual obligations.

THE IMPORTANCE OF BEING EARNEST
&
Anti-Hero

Bunburying is pretty common in Taylor's music, and we see a good example of this in "Anti-Hero". This chapter's Music Video Muse does a brilliant job showing off the two people: the real Taylor and the persona she's created, Taylor Swift™.

To draw a comparison with *The Importance of Being Earnest*, think of it this way: Taylor Swift™ is the "Ernest" persona.

In the song "Anti-Hero", Taylor suggests that the altruistic, polished and politician-like version of her that we see in public may not be the real her, but a carefully crafted image created to meet society's expectations. The music video shows this by contrasting a dressed-up version of Taylor with a more relaxed, authentic version of her who struggles to keep up with the antics of Taylor Swift™.

Just like Algernon and Jack create fake identities to live the lives they want, Taylor uses her Taylor Swift™ persona to handle the pressures of fame. This allows her to separate her true self from the demands placed on her public image.

This is her version of bunburying. She creates a persona to manage public perception while keeping her real self private.

✶ In which other songs of Taylor's do we see bunburying, or the idea of living a double life?

TAYLOR SWIFT & CLARA BOW WALK INTO A BAR

In the song "Clara Bow", Taylor mentions her own name in a way that makes you question what the name "Taylor Swift" means to you.

The song explores how people can look like famous icons, such as Clara Bow or Stevie Nicks, depending on the light they're seen in. It's about how we sometimes see people not for who they really are, but for the image they project. By including her own name in the song, Taylor is asking us to think about whether the image we have of her is the real Taylor or just a version shaped by what we expect from her.

EXPLORING IDENTITY THROUGH TAYLOR'S LYRICS

Taylor's lyrics challenge us to think about identity and perception in new ways. Use the prompts below to explore these themes in "Clara Bow" and how they connect to Taylor's experiences and to your own.

✶ Write down the names mentioned in "Clara Bow". Next to each name, make note of what comes to mind when you hear it. What do these names mean to you?

✶ Consider how the song shows these icons in different lights. How does this affect the way we see them?

✶ Why did Taylor add her own name to this list of icons? How might this connect to her balancing her public image (Taylor Swift™) with who she really is?

✦ If people saw you in different lights, which famous icons might they compare you to? How do these comparisons relate to the real you?

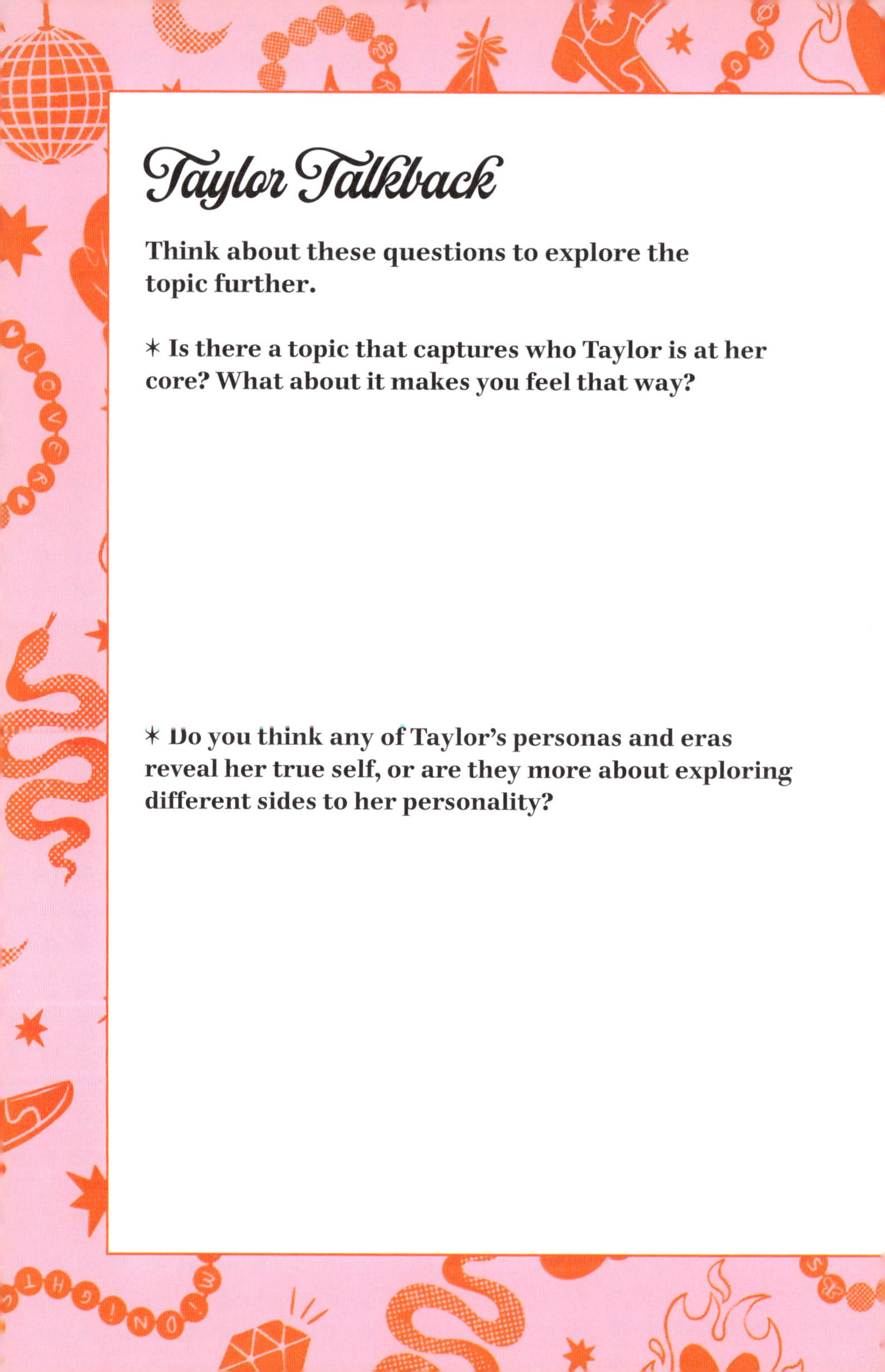

Taylor Talkback

Think about these questions to explore the topic further.

✶ Is there a topic that captures who Taylor is at her core? What about it makes you feel that way?

✶ Do you think any of Taylor's personas and eras reveal her true self, or are they more about exploring different sides to her personality?

✶ **How does Taylor's constant reinvention affect your connection to her music? Does it bring you closer to understanding her, or does it create more distance?**

CHAPTER 8

Playing the Game of Love

The complexities of love in Taylor Swift's music

THE BOOKSHELF

Rebecca
Anna Karenina

THE PLAYLIST

"tolerate it"
"Fortnight"

Queue up this chapter's songs to listen and follow along!

Exploring Love

Exploring love as a literary theme is no small feat – love is a tricky business. It's always up to something: stirring up trouble, making mischief or turning everything on its head.

For centuries, authors have used love as their secret weapon to shape character arcs, drive plot twists and reveal the rawest parts of human nature. In literature, love can be a whirlwind romance, a total disaster or something in between. So, what makes it so irresistible?

It's always changing, and it takes on a fresh meaning in every story it touches.

IT'S A LOVE STORY ... SORT OF

Taylor Swift is the *queen* of mushy love songs and the boss of breakup bops. Sure, she's got the classic "love song" thing down, but Taylor's genius is in capturing the more complicated parts of love in her lyrics.

"All Too Well (10 Minute Version)" is a ten-minute dissertation on heartbreak, misunderstanding and the emotional scars that shape us. "Dear John" reflects on messy and strained relationships and the pain that comes from manipulation. "I Can Fix Him (No Really I Can)" shows us the foolish things love makes us do and the caution we throw to the wind because of it. "Soon You'll Get Better" breaks our hearts every time because it touches on those emotional connections that go beyond romance. And "Delicate" ties all these themes together – love, identity, vulnerability and how relationships are shaped by everything around us.

Ultimately, love – whether in literature or in music – is transformative. It both brings people together and tears them apart.

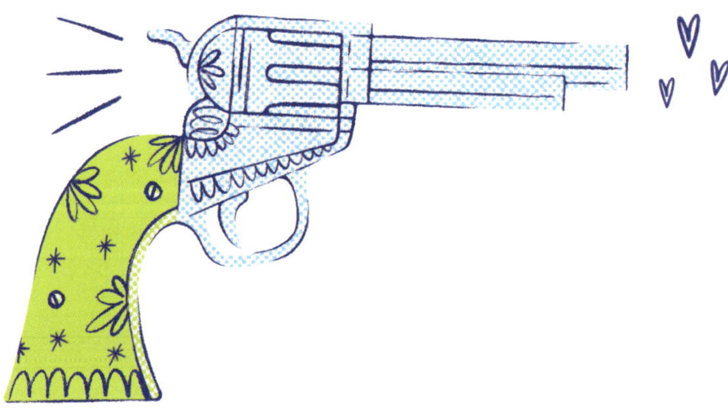

It inspires acts of heroism and acts of betrayal. And Taylor captures all of it, moving beyond the romanticism we often associate with love (see Chapter 2 for THAT side of love).

✶ How many Taylor Swift songs can you name that explore different kinds of non-romantic love?

To understand Taylor's music and lyrics, it helps to understand the complexities of love in literature. This chapter looks at how Taylor Swift's songs such as "tolerate it" and "Fortnight" reflect common themes from classic works such as *Rebecca* and *Anna Karenina*. We'll see how Taylor writes different kinds of love into her music, and you'll learn how to find the Easter eggs Taylor has hidden in each song.

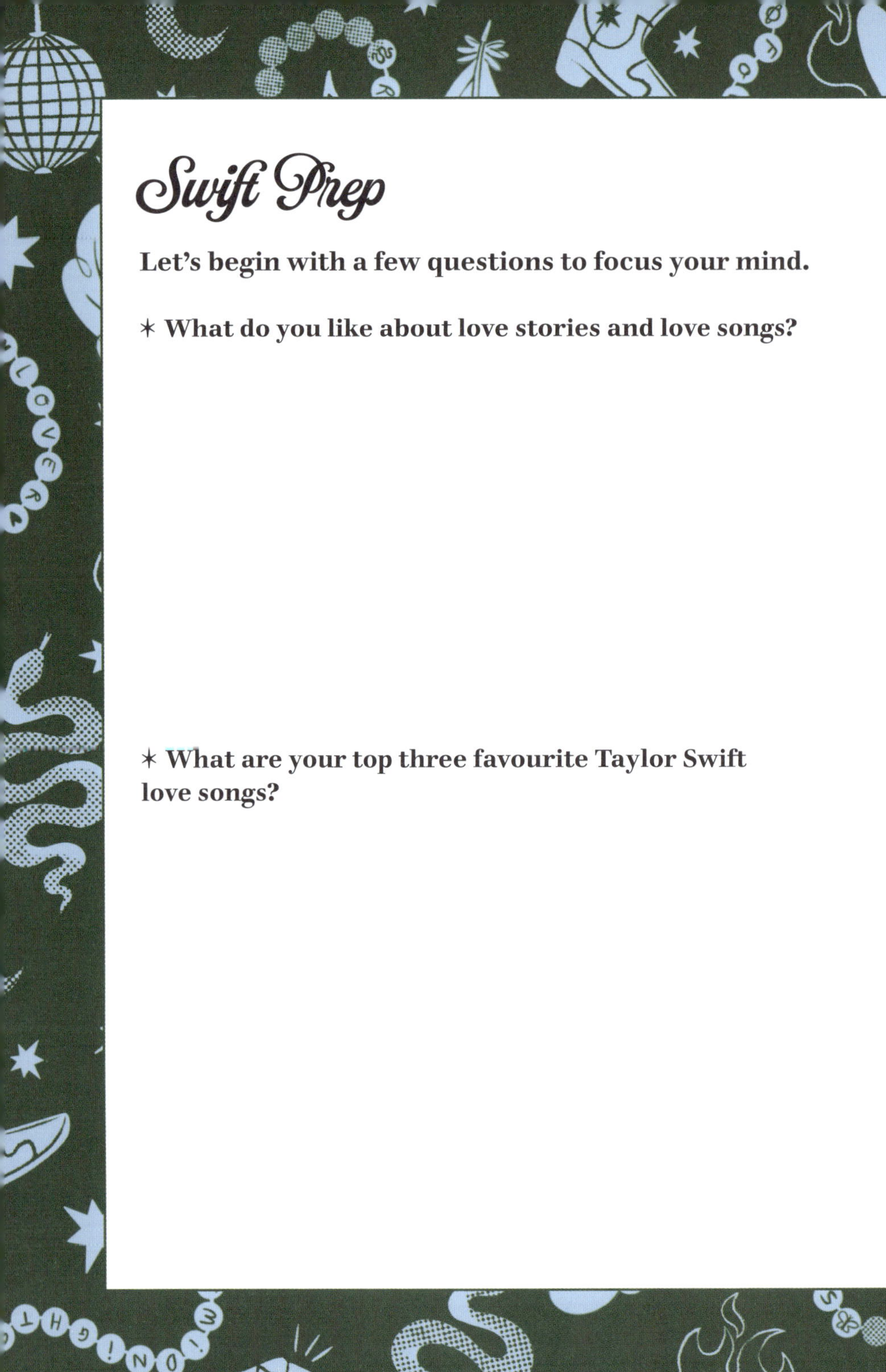

Swift Prep

Let's begin with a few questions to focus your mind.

∗ What do you like about love stories and love songs?

∗ What are your top three favourite Taylor Swift love songs?

✶ **Write a love story in five sentences or less.**

✶ **What kind of love did you write about? Did it have a happy or a sad ending? Which elements made it a love story?**

Rebecca
By Daphne du Maurier

SWIFTSNOTES

If you haven't read *Rebecca* by Daphne du Maurier yet, no biggie! Here's a quick rundown to catch you up on all the drama from this 1938 novel:

✶ A young, unnamed and unexperienced narrator looks back on her life and time at the Manderley estate. She hints at a dark and complicated past.

✶ She remembers meeting the wealthy widower Maxim de Winter while working in Monte Carlo. They quickly fall in love and he proposes. Soon, they return to his estate, Manderley.

✶ At Manderley, the new Mrs de Winter feels overshadowed by Rebecca, Maxim's dead ex-wife, who was apparently perfect and loved by everyone.

✶ The housekeeper, Mrs Danvers, is especially loyal to Rebecca, and undermines the new Mrs de Winter at every chance she gets, which isolates her and makes her insecurities worse.

✶ The authorities find a sunken boat with Rebecca's body inside, and it's revealed that Maxim killed her after she taunted him about being pregnant with another man's child, who she threatened to raise at Manderley.

✶ In the explosive finale, Manderley is set on fire. The fire was likely caused by Mrs Danvers, who was devastated by Rebecca's death.

REBECCA
&
tolerate it

Taylor told Apple Music in an interview that "tolerate it" from her *evermore* album was directly inspired by Maxim and Mrs de Winter's relationship in *Rebecca.* She related to the way in which the narrator bends over backward to earn her husband's love but is overshadowed and merely tolerated because of the constant presence of his first wife.

Out of context, some of the lyrics from this *evermore* track sound like they're about a child trying to please a disapproving parent who doesn't agree with their choices in love. This makes sense considering that Mrs de Winter is treated like a child throughout *Rebecca* – emphasized by the fact that Maxim is about 20 years older than her. It certainly doesn't help that Maxim leaves her waiting alone in the house for hours or entire afternoons without telling her where he's gone or when he'll return, or frequently brushes off her concerns, which makes her feel even more insignificant.

✶ Which lyrics from "tolerate it" best capture the dynamic of one person being seen as younger or less mature in a relationship?

BURNING DOWN THE LOVER HOUSE

During her Eras Tour, Taylor burns down the *Lover* house in her concert visuals. The house, born from her "Lover" music video, features rooms in different colours that represent each of her past albums and eras.

✶ **Does this remind you of anything that happens in *Rebecca*?**

In the novel, the Manderley fire symbolizes more than one big idea. First, it marks the end of Rebecca's influence – her presence was everywhere, and the fire finally breaks that hold. It's also a total cleanse! The fire wipes away old secrets and baggage that Maxim and the new Mrs de Winter were stuck carrying, giving them a chance to start afresh. It also serves as an emotional release and a dramatic end to all the tension that had been building up after the truth about Rebecca came out. Finally, for Mrs Danvers, the fire is pure revenge – maybe even *better* than revenge. If she can't keep the house, no one can.

Whether it was intentional or not, Taylor's decision to burn down the *Lover* house may carry a lot of the same meaning as the fire at Manderley.

✶ What do you think burning down the *Lover* house in Taylor's Eras Tour visuals symbolizes?

Anna Karenina
By Leo Tolstoy

SWIFTSNOTES

Listen, if you haven't read all 800 pages of *Anna Karenina*, we get it. Here is a crash course on Leo Tolstoy's novel from 1878:

✶ Anna Karenina is a married noblewoman who meets the dashing Count Vronsky at a train station. Sparks fly, despite her being married to the serious Alexei Karenin.

✶ Word gets out about their affair, and it becomes a public scandal. While Vronsky's reputation takes a small hit, Anna is judged more harshly by society.

✶ Her husband refuses to divorce her, which traps Anna in a messy and complicated situation.

✶ Meanwhile, Konstantin Levin, a friend of Anna's husband and brother, navigates his own struggles with love and purpose in rural Russia. He eventually marries Kitty Shcherbatsky.

✶ As Anna's relationship with lover Vronsky becomes strained and she becomes more isolated, she struggles under the weight of society's rejection.

✶ Unable to cope, Anna throws herself under a train, while Levin's story wraps up with him finding purpose and contentment though his love for Kitty, the birth of their child and a renewed faith in life – a slight contrast to Anna's fate.

ANNA KARENINA & *Fortnight*

The reason *Anna Karenina* has remained such a significant classic love story over the years has a lot to do with its deeply human characters and the intense emotions they feel and act upon.

Taylor Swift captures those same deep, sometimes irrational, emotions in her music, especially when it comes to heartbreak. Take *The Tortured Poets Department* – the entire 31-song anthology explores different psychological states and unpacks everything love puts you through.

During the album's rollout, some Swifties predicted it would follow the five stages of grief – denial, anger, bargaining, depression and acceptance – following the "death" of a relationship, based on the era's shades-of-greige aesthetic.

The album's exploration of intense emotions kicks off right from its first song and single, "Fortnight", featuring Post Malone.

Aside from giving the old English slang for "two weeks" a modern comeback, the song captures the fleeting passion of a relationship comparable to Anna and Vronsky's affair, complete with the devastation left behind. Some might call this a "situationship" – and if you've ever been in one, you know that the heartbreak can stick around long after it has finished.

WELL, WELL, WELL ...
IF IT ISN'T THE CONSEQUENCES OF MY OWN ACTIONS

Now that the word "fortnight" is back in our vocabulary, we can see how this is contrasted with the word "forever" in the chorus of the song, emphasizing how short the relationship Taylor sings about really was. Yet the emotional intensity of it gives it a timeless feel.

Similarly, in *Anna Karenina*, Tolstoy describes how Vronsky avoids looking at Anna, "as if she were the sun". This comparison illustrates the allure and danger of their relationship – beautiful but ultimately destructive.

Both the song and the novel show how fleeting passion can feel all-consuming, and it comes with some inevitable consequences.

✶ What scenes or visuals in the "Fortnight" music video capture the fleeting, "here today, gone tomorrow" nature of the relationship Taylor Swift and Post Malone both sing about?

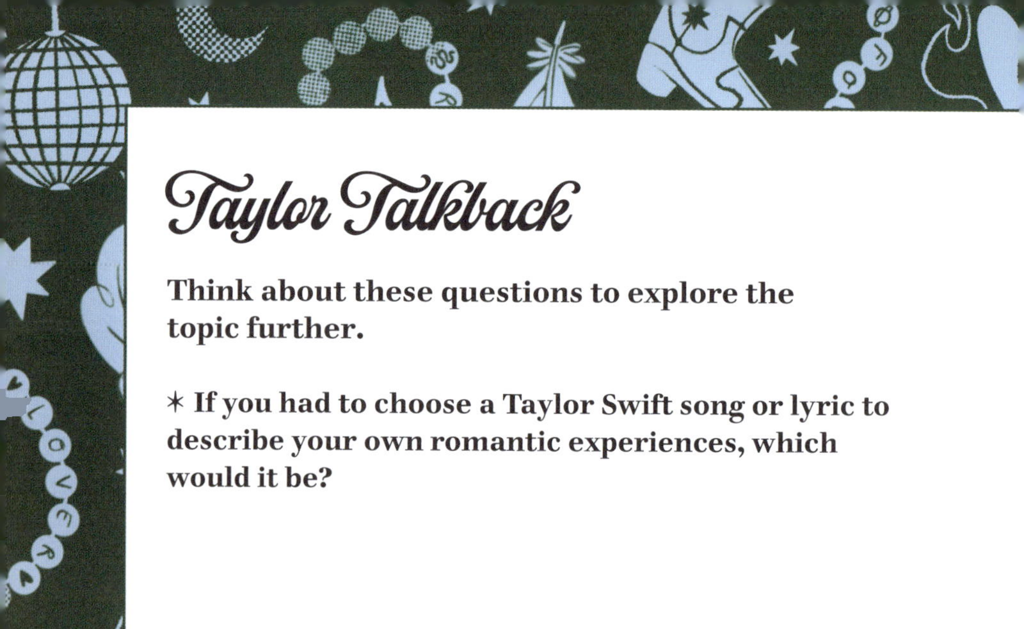

Taylor Talkback

Think about these questions to explore the topic further.

✶ If you had to choose a Taylor Swift song or lyric to describe your own romantic experiences, which would it be?

✶ Which symbols does Taylor Swift use in her music to represent love? What do you think they mean?

✶ **How have you seen Taylor's interpretation of love change throughout her different eras?**

CHAPTER 9
The Monster on the Hill

The gothic elements revealed in Taylor Swift's music

THE BOOKSHELF	THE PLAYLIST
Frankenstein	**"The Alchemy"** **"Who's Afraid of Little Old Me?"**

Queue up this chapter's songs to listen and follow along!

Gothic Tales

Gothic literature is more than just spooky stories of angsty characters dressed in black. It's all about exploring the eerie and unknown, and the unsettling feelings these things give us.

Gothic tales stand out for their mysterious settings in old castles and foggy forests. They include supernatural elements – like ghosts, monsters or strange events – that blur the line between real and imaginary. The characters are usually misunderstood, which makes them feel afraid or causes others to fear them, leading to despair or even madness. Villains use their power to create danger for others, and the main character is usually a tragic hero, flawed in a way that leads to their own downfall.

But what truly defines Gothic literature is that it's reactionary. The genre popped up in the late 1700s during the Industrial Revolution, which was a time of social, political and economic upheaval. Technology and manufacturing rapidly transformed the workplace and daily life.

Gothic literature gave a voice to the fears and anxieties people felt about the changing world. It turned those worries into stories and forced readers to confront their deep-seated fears about industrial progress, the unknown future and how life was morphing around them.

To understand Taylor's music and lyrics, it helps to understand Gothic literature. This chapter looks at how Taylor Swift's songs such as "The Alchemy" and "Who's Afraid of Little Old Me?" reflect common themes from classic works, such as *Frankenstein*. We'll see how Taylor writes Gothic elements into her music, and you'll learn how to find the Easter eggs Taylor has hidden in each song.

Let's begin with a few questions to focus your mind.

∗ What comes to mind when you hear the word "gothic"?

∗ As she has grown up, Taylor has released songs with darker themes. How do these songs compare to some of Taylor's lighter, more radio-friendly songs, such as "Shake It Off" and "22"?

✶ How do the mysterious settings in Taylor's music videos for songs like "willow" or "Look What You Made Me Do" affect your mood compared to her brighter, upbeat videos for songs like "You Belong With Me" or "ME!"?

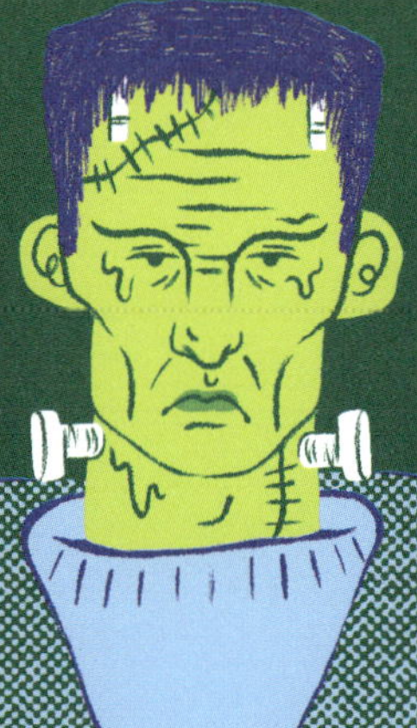

Frankenstein

By Mary Shelley

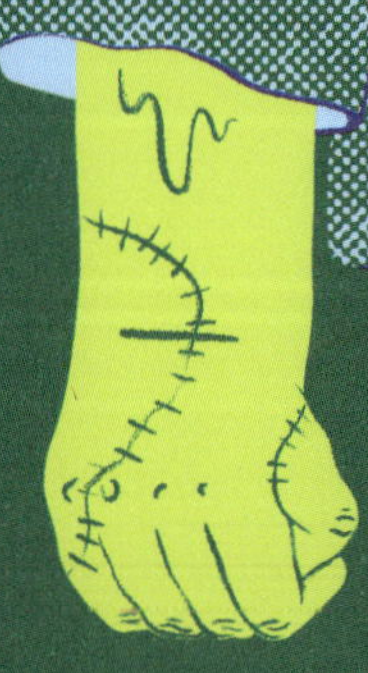

SWIFTSNOTES

You're not familiar with the quintessential 1818 Gothic story of *Frankenstein*? That's okay! Here is a quick rundown:

✶ Victor Frankenstein is a young scientist obsessed with decay. He stitches together body parts he acquires from graveyards and brings a creature to life.

✶ Victor is horrified by his creation, so he leaves the creature to fend for himself. The creature tries to fit in with society, but he is constantly rejected and mistreated because of how ugly he is.

✶ Over time, the creature gets smarter. He learns to speak and read, and after some people-watching, he confronts Victor and asks for a girlfriend to help ease his loneliness.

✶ Victor agrees at first, but then freaks out and destroys the female creature, afraid he might create a race of monsters.

✶ The creature is *not* happy. He vows revenge and goes on a rampage to kill Victor's closest loved ones, including his BFF and, on their wedding night, his bride.

✶ Victor takes the creature to the Arctic and eventually dies from exhaustion. The creature, surprisingly heartbroken, mourns his creator and disappears into the icy wilderness to end his life.

FRANKENSTEIN & *The Alchemy*

Victor Frankenstein grew up in a family that valued knowledge, which fuelled his curiosity about life and death and led him to a little thing called "alchemy" – a magical science focused on transformation and creation. He was convinced that alchemy would unlock the secret of life, and his obsession led him to create the "Frankenstein" monster.

In her song "The Alchemy", Taylor Swift reflects on her own transformation – moving on from the expectations that society has placed on her, first as America's country-singing sweetheart, then as a glitter-wearing, red-lipped pop star, and later as a so-called man-eating industry snake.

The song puts into writing how much she loves taking control of her image, reinventing herself from era to era – so much so that it intoxicates her, like white wine.

✶ How do you handle change and transformation in your life, particularly as you grow older or take on new roles?

In *Frankenstein*, Victor's obsession is with alchemy and creating life. His focus isn't on what he creates, but on pushing the boundaries of science to prove his own intelligence. This tracks, considering he abandons the creature to survive on his own – it shows he never thought or cared about the outcome of his experiment.

And while Taylor is no mad scientist, like Victor, she shares a similar love for the process of transformation.

Take verse one of "The Alchemy": Taylor sings about coming back stronger after a tough time. It's in present tense with an active voice, showing us that she is intoxicated by the process of coming back and transforming, not just by the end result.

We get the feeling that Taylor enjoys reinventing herself so much that it doesn't even matter what people think of her on the other side, which is similar to Victor's indifference around what happens to his creation.

✶ Which transition between Taylor Swift's eras surprised you the most? Why?

✶ Do you think Taylor intends to surprise her audience with her transitions to new eras, or are they just a natural part of her growth?

FRANKENSTEIN

&

Who's Afraid of Little Old Me?

"The Alchemy" casts Taylor as Victor Frankenstein, but "Who's Afraid of Little Old Me?" writes her into a different role entirely – this time as the creature!

In the song's bridge, Taylor gives us the classic Gothic feeling of being misunderstood as she experiences a similar kind of isolation from society that the creature experiences in *Frankenstein*. The lyrics paint a picture of someone who feels trapped, ridiculed and exiled to a sort of emotional "asylum".

"Who's Afraid Of Little Old Me?" mirrors the creature's solitude and emotional despair, particularly when he watches a family – the De Laceys – through their cottage window. He learns about human relationships and emotions by observing them and realises how much he longs to be part of a world that will never accept him.

Does this remind you of any other Taylor Swift songs? "I Look in People's Windows" from *The Tortured Poets Department* also captures that sense of Gothic isolation, being on the outside looking in.

✶ What other Taylor Swift songs capture the Gothic idea of being alienated from society?

Continuing with the theme of being misunderstood, Taylor's lyrics in "Who's Afraid Of Little Old Me?" reflect how society mistreats her – far beyond what anyone should have to endure. From overt criticism and death threats to relentless scrutiny, she's constantly on display, picked apart and judged. She snarls at how this treatment has disturbed her over the years, forcing her to grow an outer shell so tough that she now appears almost monster-like to those who don't truly understand her.

It's a similar story in *Frankenstein*, where the creature starts off wanting to connect with others but is immediately rejected because of his appearance. His loneliness and misery come from being misjudged by society. At one point, he says, "I was benevolent and good; misery made me a fiend" – a line that could easily belong in "Who's Afraid Of Little Old Me".

✶ Which lyric in "Who's Afraid of Little Old Me?" reminds you of the creature's experiences in *Frankenstein*?

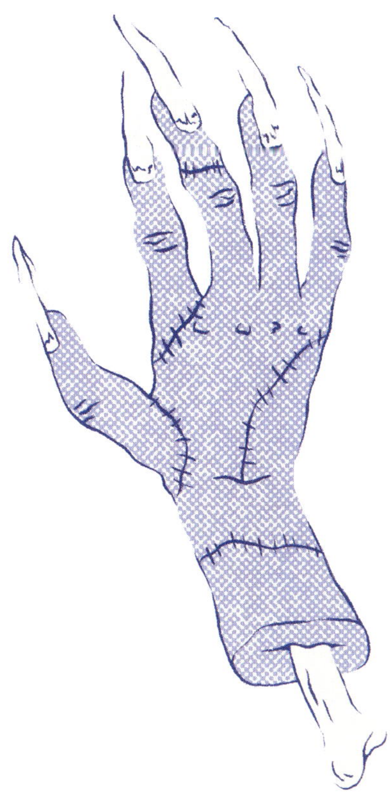

Taylor Talkback

Think about these questions to explore the topic further.

✶ Are there any Gothic themes in Taylor Swift's other songs?

✶ What do you like or dislike about Taylor's darker, more Gothic-themed songs compared to her lighter, playful "glitter gel pen" tracks, as she calls them?

✶ **Based on the narrative she has crafted in her songs, who do you think Taylor identifies with more, Victor Frankenstein or the creature he creates? Why?**

CHAPTER 10

The End of an Era

Exploring how Taylor Swift's music can be further analysed through a literary lens

Queue up this chapter's songs to listen and follow along!

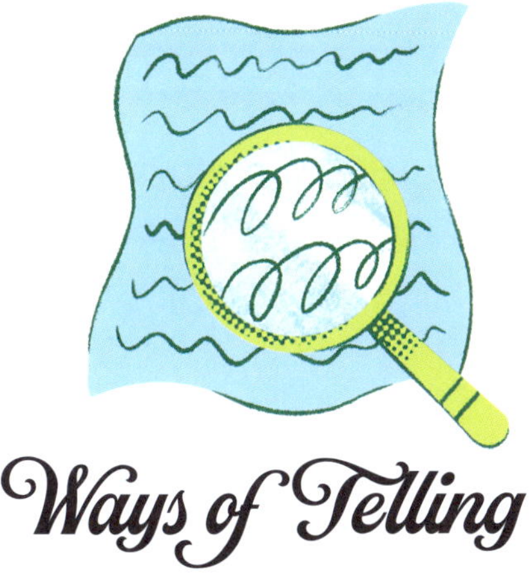

Ways of Telling

Think back (or flip back) to nine chapters ago, where this book first started. The song "Dear Reader" had us calling Taylor Swift the ultimate unreliable narrator. It was riddled with contradictions, hidden secrets and truths that felt far from reality, and we questioned how far we could trust Taylor's storytelling. Can we take her lyrics at face value, or is there always something more beneath the surface?

Throughout this book, we've explored the many ways that Taylor's music mirrors the stories we grew up reading and the literary techniques they made famous, from *bildungsroman* to Gothicism. Yet the theme of the unreliable narrator has remained a thread from the beginning.

Taylor may not always give us the full truth in her lyrics – and that's the point. She is inviting us to look deeper and to uncover the meaning of her music for ourselves.

To understand Taylor's music and lyrics, it helps to understand the way she plays with storytelling. In "The Manuscript", she asks us to look at her work differently – as if we're revisiting an old draft of a finished story. We'll discover how Taylor uses this metaphor to explore her past, and how it shapes her music, and you'll learn how the stories she tells continue to evolve once they're shared with the world.

Let's begin with a few questions to focus your mind.

✶ Is there a certain literary character or story that you think best correlates with a Taylor Swift song? What connections come to mind between the themes, emotions or arcs in the story and the song's lyrics?

✶ If you could see the manuscript or original draft of one Taylor Swift song, which song would it be, and why?

✶ Taylor Swift loves revisiting and referencing her old songs in her newer works. What is your favourite example of this? How does the repetition add to the meaning of both songs?

WHAT IS A MANUSCRIPT?

A manuscript is an author's first or early draft of a work. Reading a manuscript can give you a peek behind the curtain at the raw creation before it became a finished piece.

Manuscripts are central to a genre called the epistolary format, where stories are told through letters, diary entries and personal documents. This approach makes the stories feel more personal and real, and we see this in the books *Dracula* and *Frankenstein*, as well as in some of Taylor's songs.

THE MANUSCRIPT

In "The Manuscript", Taylor looks back at a past relationship, almost like she's reading the pages of an old diary. The song talks about memories and emotions from that time in the same way a memoir would.

✶ Which lyric or lyrics from "The Manuscript" sound like pages straight from Taylor Swift's diary?

✶ How does the format or storytelling style of "The Manuscript" add to its epistolary feel?

We could see the relationship she reflects on as a metaphor for her entire body of work. Taylor often revisits and reworks old songs and stories into her newer works, in the same way that someone might look back on the memories and emotions of a past relationship. Do you see how she repeats the word "midnight" with the same cadence in "New Year's Day" and "Paris", and how she reuses the same piano medley in "champagne problems" and "Chloe or Sam or Sophia or Marcus"? These motifs reflect the way that she takes personal moments and transforms them into public art.

The idea of revisiting a manuscript relates to how fans engage with Taylor's music. Just as the narrator of "The Manuscript" looks back on their story, and as Taylor revisits old songs in new works, we find ourselves returning to her music and discovering new meanings. It's an ongoing conversation. Her music grows as we do.

IF IT ISN'T TAYLOR'S, WHOSE IS IT?

Listen carefully to those final moments of "The Manuscript". Taylor reflects on revisiting the manuscript – of her entire body of work – but she realises that the stories in her songs don't just belong to her anymore. Once she shares her memories as art, she has no control over how they are interpreted. We fans and critics find our own meanings in her lyrics and Easter eggs – ones that make sense to us!

✶ Which lyrics in "The Manuscript" show us that Taylor is reflecting on her songwriting process?

There are many ways to look at Taylor's music: through her muses, her personal life or her musical influences, such as The Beatles, Stevie Nicks and Elvis. In this book, we've been using literature as a tool to find thought-provoking references and literary connections in Taylor's storytelling, helping you explore her work on a more intimate and reflective level.

FROM TAYLOR'S HANDS TO YOURS

In "Dear Reader", Taylor encourages you to find your own meaning in her music, and as you've moved through each chapter, you've done just that – uncovering concealed stories and themes beneath the surface. By looking at her lyrics as literary texts, you've learned to read between the lines and find the hidden references and narratives.

In "The Manuscript", Taylor reflects on how her stories evolve once they're shared with the world. Like an author revisiting a draft, she reinterprets her own work. But she also acknowledges that the meaning comes from, as the song suggests, the actors and dancers who interact with it.

Through a literary lens, you've seen how her music isn't just personal to her – once her stories have been shared, they become shaped by everyone who listens. This is part of what makes the Taylor's Versions – the rerecordings of her first six albums – so special. They invite us to revisit, reinterpret and discover new connections in her songs that we might not have noticed before.

This book has always been about more than just Taylor Swift's music; it's about storytelling. As Taylor continues to create and share her art, new songs, stories and Easter eggs will be waiting to be found. So, keep wondering about, analysing and finding the clues and connections that speak to you.

And as you continue to explore Taylor's work, remember: the story isn't just hers anymore ... it's yours too.

Taylor Talkback

Let's end with a few questions to reflect on what you learned.

∗ How has looking at Taylor's music through a literary lens changed the way you listen to her songs compared to when you first picked up this book?

✶ How has learning about narrative techniques such as the unreliable narrator, coming-of-age stories (*bildungsroman*), dual identities (bunburying) or the epistolary format deepened your appreciation of Taylor Swift's music? In which songs have you found these techniques to have been especially effective or meaningful?

✶ Do you think art still belongs to the artist once it's out in the world? Why, or why not?

✶ If you could connect one of Taylor Swift's songs to a book we didn't cover here, which one would it be, and why?

✶ Which storytelling tool do you think Taylor Swift uses to best effect in her songs?

✶ If Taylor Swift's eras were chapters in a book, how would you describe each one? How do they all connect to tell her story?

✶ **If you could ask Taylor Swift one question about how she writes her music, what would it be?**

✶ **Which Taylor Swift song do you think would make a great novel? Why?**

✶ **What do you love most about analysing Taylor Swift's music? What about analysing it through a literary lens?**

✶ How has this book inspired you to connect Taylor's music to other forms of art, such as films, paintings or TV shows?

Acknowledgements

This book would not exist without Whitney Butler – my gracious, encouraging and always-smiling partner who taught me to "follow my joy" and gave me the support, safety and space to do just that. Thank you for sitting on the hallway floor with me until the wee hours of the morning, discussing lyric interpretations of Taylor Swift's music, and for never making me feel silly for unapologetically loving every second of it. Thank you for being my sounding board for our Dear Reader classes and for creating the most beautiful, intricate presentations to go with each lesson. Most of all, thank you for loving me. It's amazing what you can accomplish when you're filled with a love like the kind you give.

To Amy Collins: thank you for finding the Dear Reader course and letting it lead you to me, and for always believing in the ability of my star to rise. This is my first book, and the process was so different from any journalistic work I've done. Because of that, I'm endlessly grateful for your patience, encouragement and unwavering belief in the impact this book could have. From the very start, you saw the community this book could reach, and I'll forever treasure our first phone call where you rattled off terms and deadlines like we'd been working together for years (I was terrified, by the way). Your forwardness inspires me.

To my team of editors, Sophie Blackman and Ella Chappell: thank you for being the extra set of eyes and the steady hands this book needed. Your feedback, encouragement and care for a topic that means so much to such a large and passionate community of people made all the difference, and I'm so grateful to have had you on this (very fast) journey.

I want to thank a handful of my USC graduate professors: Paula Mejia, for guiding me through my first published analysis of Taylor Swift's music. The work I created under your leadership and editing was the catalyst for the Dear Reader class, community and everything that fills these pages. To Oscar Garza, for pushing me to channel my thoughts, feelings and experiences into my writing as a way to connect with others. And to Alan Abrahamson: I'll never forget when you told me, "I love to watch the way your brain works." You always encouraged me to share my perspective, no matter how unexpected it was, and you never tired of me finding ways to bring Taylor Swift into our law and sports classes – places she definitely didn't belong. You reminded me that critiques of my work are not critiques of my character, a lesson that has greatly helped me. You also taught me to cut through the noise, focus on what makes me happy and trust what feels right.

To April Previte Turner, my sixth-grade language arts teacher, and the first person who ever told me I was a good writer: I'll never forget the day you dressed as a cat and sang along to the *Cats* musical soundtrack, all to teach your students how to analyse poetic devices in music. What you taught me then has stayed with me and helped shape how I've analysed Taylor Swift's music for this book.

To my Dear Reader class, especially MK Rockett, Jaime Alverson, LeAnne Rowley, Natasha Martinez, Katie Lusardi, Katie Kornreich, Savannah Cupples, Jacqueline Reeves, Paige Thurmond, Allie Wells, Emily Malott and so many others:

I had no idea how much I needed you or your friendship when I started Dear Reader. I couldn't have imagined the kind of community that would come from following something I loved. You've opened my eyes to new interpretations of Taylor's music and art far beyond anything I could have imagined. Thank you for your brilliance, your creativity and your passion in every class and every conversation we've had since the start of this journey.

And finally, this wouldn't be a book inspired by the brilliant work of Taylor Swift without acknowledging Taylor herself. Taylor: I don't know if you'll ever see this book, but if you do, I want you to know that I see you. No, I don't know you personally, but I see and respect you as an artist, as an incredibly intelligent woman with dynamic experiences to draw from and as someone who uses her work to connect so deeply with others. I see your work not just as stories about muses or headlines, but as carefully crafted art that reflects your experience while speaking to mine – and countless others' – in the way I think you intended. Thank you, Taylor, for being vulnerable and for putting your art out into the world. The community you've created through your work is extraordinary, and I'm grateful every day to be a part of it.

About the Author

Viktoria Capek is the brains behind the viral Dear Reader course and is a celebrated journalist, arts and culture writer, and events producer. Her number one passion is building community.

She was widely recognised as the first openly queer local news personality in Arkansas, US, where Viktoria used her platform to address issues such as gender wage gaps and the underrepresentation of QTBIPOC individuals in broadcasting, which resonated with a worldwide audience. Her candid social media posts – where she shared her journey of leaving broadcast news – grew her online community tremendously.

Viktoria is currently the Director of Communications at the Venture Center in Little Rock, and the programme lead for VCWoman Achieve, a mentorship programme supporting women and non-binary entrepreneurs. Beyond her role at the Venture Center, she manages media for the Athena Film Festival in New York City, organizes pro-education events such as I READ BANNED BOOKS and she co-founded Hairpins, a monthly pop-up event for queer women in the South.

Viktoria holds a master's degree in arts journalism from the University of Southern California's Annenberg School, where she served as arts editor for *Ampersand* and received a National Arts and Entertainment Journalism Award for her cultural commentary writing. Through her work, writing and event production, Viktoria remains dedicated to uplifting women, people of colour and the LGBTQ+ community.

References

INTRODUCTION

* "Taylor Swift Interview: Life Lessons", *Women's Health*, 2008, womenshealthmag.com/life/a19982986/taylor-swift-interview/
* *Vogue*, "73 Questions With Taylor Swift", YouTube, 9:41, 19 April 2016, youtube.com/watch?v=XnbCSboujF4
* Elle UK, "Taylor Swift on Pop Music and How Songwriting Became Her 'Weapon'", *Elle*, 2019, elle.com/uk/life-and-culture/a26546099/taylor-swift-pop-music/

CHAPTER 1: Taylor Swift as the Ultimate Unreliable Narrator

* Fitzgerald, F. Scott, *The Great Gatsby*, Scribner, New York, 1925, p.17
* Fitzgerald, F. Scott, *The Great Gatsby*, Scribner, New York, 1925, p.7

Chapter 2: A Modern-Day Romantic Poet

* Shakespeare, William, "Romeo and Juliet", act 2, scene 1, *The Complete Works of Shakespeare*, Oxford University Press, Oxford, 1938, p.254
* Shakespeare, William, "Romeo and Juliet", act 1, scene 5, *The Complete Works of Shakespeare*, Oxford University Press, Oxford, 1938, p.252
* Brontë, Emily, *Wuthering Heights*, Aerie, New York, 1848, p.184

Chapter 3: Growing Up & Getting Old

* Barrie, J.M., *Peter and Wendy*, Scribner, New York, 1911, p.3
* Barrie, J.M., *Peter and Wendy*, Scribner, New York, 1911, p.1
* Lee, Harper, *To Kill a Mockingbird*, Warner Books, New York, 1982, p.215

Chapter 4: The 21st-Century Feminist

* Maxim, "Taylor Swift Tops 2015 Maxim Hot 100", 2015, maxim.com
* Plath, Sylvia, *The Bell Jar*, Bantam Books, New York, 1981, p.77

Chapter 5: Rebel With a Cause

* Miller, Arthur, *The Crucible*, Penguin Group, New York, 1976, p.116
* Miller, Arthur, *The Crucible*, Penguin Group, New York, 1976, p.141

Chapter 8: Playing the Game of Love

* "Taylor Swift: Apple Music Awards Interview," Apple Music, 2020
* Tolstoy, Leo, *Anna Karenina*, Barnes & Noble Books, New York, 1997, p.27

Chapter 9: The Monster on the Hill

* Shelley, Mary, *Frankenstein*, Tom Doherty Associates, New York, 1988, p.96
* "Taylor Swift Reveals Her Writing Process In Nashville Songwriter Awards Speech", *The Hollywood Reporter*, 2022, hollywoodreporter.com

Notes

Notes

The story of Watkins began in 1893, when scholar of esotericism John Watkins founded our bookshop, inspired by the lament of his friend and teacher Madame Blavatsky that there was nowhere in London to buy books on mysticism, occultism or metaphysics. That moment marked the birth of Watkins, soon to become the publisher of many of the leading lights of spiritual literature, including Carl Jung, Rudolf Steiner, Alice Bailey and Chögyam Trungpa.

Today, the passion at Watkins Publishing for vigorous questioning is still resolute. Our stimulating and groundbreaking list ranges from ancient traditions and complementary medicine to the latest ideas about personal development, holistic wellbeing and consciousness exploration. We remain at the cutting edge, committed to publishing books that change lives.

DISCOVER MORE AT:

www.watkinspublishing.com

Read our blog

Watch and listen to our authors in action

Sign up to our mailing list

We celebrate conscious, passionate, wise and happy living.

Be part of that community by visiting

/watkinspublishing 

/watkinsbooks